Leading Special Education

How to Support,

Retain, and

Empower Teachers

for Success

BREAUNA C. WALL

foreword by Anthony Muhammad

Solution Tree | Press

Copyrxight © 2025 by Solution Tree Press

Materials appearing here are copyrighted. With one exception, all rights are reserved. Readers may reproduce only those pages marked "Reproducible." Otherwise, no part of this book may be reproduced or transmitted in any form or by any means (electronic, photocopying, recording, or otherwise) without prior written permission of the publisher.

555 North Morton Street
Bloomington, IN 47404
800.733.6786 (toll free) / 812.336.7700
FAX: 812.336.7790

email: info@SolutionTree.com
SolutionTree.com
Visit **go.SolutionTree.com/specialneeds** to download the free reproducibles in this book.

Printed in the United States of America

Library of Congress Cataloging-in-Publication Data

Names: Wall, Breauna C., author.
Title: Leading special education : how to support, retain, and empower teachers for success / Breauna C. Wall.
Description: Bloomington, IN : Solution Tree Press, [2025] | Includes bibliographical references and index.
Identifiers: LCCN 2024047841 (print) | LCCN 2024047842 (ebook) | ISBN 9781962188739 (paperback) | ISBN 9781962188746 (ebook)
Subjects: LCSH: Special education. | Special education teachers.
Classification: LCC LC3965 .W26 2025 (print) | LCC LC3965 (ebook) | DDC 371.9--dc23/eng/20250402
LC record available at https://lccn.loc.gov/2024047841
LC ebook record available at https://lccn.loc.gov/2024047842

Solution Tree
Jeffrey C. Jones, CEO
Edmund M. Ackerman, President

Solution Tree Press
President and Publisher: Douglas M. Rife
Associate Publishers: Todd Brakke and Kendra Slayton
Editorial Director: Laurel Hecker
Art Director: Rian Anderson
Copy Chief: Jessi Finn
Production Editor: Madonna Evans
Copy Editor: Anne Marie Watkins
Proofreader: Elijah Oates
Text and Cover Designer: Laura Cox
Acquisitions Editors: Carol Collins and Hilary Goff
Content Development Specialist: Amy Rubenstein
Associate Editors: Sarah Ludwig and Elijah Oates
Editorial Assistant: Madison Chartier

Acknowledgments

I found this section to be one of the most challenging to write. Honoring others is a way of life for me. God has blessed me with an incredible support system. There are people who have been heavily involved in my life and others I've had brief connections with who have made lasting impacts on my writing journey.

Jesus Christ is the way, the truth, and the life. God, the father, is my leading light, my constant, my everything. His gifts, grace, and almightiness made this book possible.

To all my family—you have a firm foundation in my heart. To my mom, Suheir, who has been an unwavering support in my life and a cheerleader of this book. Thank you for filling the room with laughter and loving with your whole heart. To my father, who calls me "Dr. Little Love,"—thank you for loving me unconditionally and for being specially placed in my heart forever. To my dad, Chico, who passed away before I began this writing journey but contributed greatly to the person I am today, making it possible, through God, for me to have the discipline and resilience to write this book. To Celeste and Coach—thank you for your unconditional love, prayers, and support. To my brothers and sisters—there is so much to say here. You know who you are and the impact each of you has had on my life. Thank you for believing in me, encouraging me, supporting me, laughing with me, and loving me!

To my daughter and son—you have a central place in my life now and forever. Your unconditional love is a constant motivation and joy in my life.

Writing this book is possible because of the love you surround me with. Thank you for always seeing the best in me and believing in me.

To my best friends—Christina, instantly a smile grows across my face with misty eyes. You are my friend, my laugh-partner, my pick-me up, my twin. Thank you for being all of who you are. For chasing God with me, loving me, encouraging me, and celebrating me. You literally give the *best* hugs! I look forward to a lifetime with you.

Chalonne, my girl. The first thing that comes to mind when I close my eyes and reminisce is the *Donkey Kong* theme song and us dancing down Xerxes Avenue. I have been blessed to know you most of my life and am honored to spend the rest of it in friendship with you. A huge thank-you for spending all hours of the day with me on Zoom and FaceTime while I wrote the final chapters of this book.

Tavarski Wallace, my friend—thank you for your infinite support, encouragement, and friendship. We've gone on to co-host *The Straight Ed Talks Podcast* and have a lifetime to go! I thank God for connecting us.

To Lindsay Scacco—our life journey began as colleagues, and through God it's evolved into a beautiful friendship between us and our children. Cheers to many years in friendship.

To all my friends who have prayed with me, encouraged me, advised me, and supported me in this lifetime—thank you.

To Mr. T (Todd Wade) and the Pan-American Charter School family—thank you for being the start of my career in education, for trusting me to ignite positive change in our school community, and for always fostering a sense of belonging, unity, and constant growth.

Dr. Anthony Muhammad—thank you for being a friend and an admirable leader in education. Thank you for choosing to share your gifts with the world and with me. Your book *Transforming School Culture* positively influenced my work as a school leader and it is an honor now to call you friend. Thank you for believing in my value in this field and giving me a seat at several tables.

To Dr. Mary Rice—you have been a special blessing in my life. Thank you for being a leader in online studies championing for our diverse learners and educators. Thank you for being a critical part of my research journey, for guiding me, believing in me, and empowering me!

Dr. Keri Guilbault—thank you for mentoring me, publishing with me, presenting with me, and trusting me to lead doctoral students in research and practice. I value you immensely.

Dr. Shinay Bowman—thank you for championing me, investing in me, and allowing our God-sent connection to grow. You are a gem in this world, and I am blessed call you friend.

To Christina, Lindsay, Erika, Nicole, Sharon, Ariel, Jorge ("J"), and Amanda—thank you for sharing your lived experiences and contributing to this book. Each of you is a champion in this field, and I sincerely appreciate your commitment to collaboration and continuous development.

To my acquisitions editor at Solution Tree, Hilary Goff—I remember the day as if it were yesterday that you reached out to me. The impact of your initiating that connection will go on to have a profound impact in this world, not only on myself and my family but on countless others. Thank you for encouraging me and guiding me through this journey.

Finally, to Solution Tree—thank you for seeing the value in my contribution and partnering with me in this book journey.

Solution Tree Press would like to thank the following reviewers:

John D. Ewald
Educator, Consultant,
Speaker, Teacher
Frederick, Maryland

Jenna Fanshier
Principal
Marion Elementary School
Marion, Kansas

Louis Lim
Principal
Bur Oak Secondary School
Markham, Ontario, Canada

Janel Ross
Principal
White River School District
Buckley, Washington

Visit **go.SolutionTree.com/specialneeds** to download the free reproducibles in this book.

Table of Contents

About the Author xi

Foreword xiii

Introduction 1
    Why I Wrote This Book 2
    What's in This Book 4

Chapter One
Retaining Special Educators Through Systems of Support 7
    Improving Relationships and Culture With Mentorship 9
    Understanding the Power of Connections 27
    Building Bridges Through Effective Communication 27
    Tips From the Top 28
    Voices From the Field 29
    Takeaway Tool Kit 31
    Wrap-Up 35

Chapter Two
Investing in Professional Learning 37
    The Ongoing Professional Learning Framework 38
    Job-Embedded Training 54
    Tips From the Top 57
    Voices From the Field 59
    Takeaway Tool Kit 60
    Wrap-Up 60

Chapter Three
Co-Teaching and Co-Planning 63
- Co-Teaching: Collaborating Through Collective Pedagogy 65
- Co-Planning: Bringing Educators Together to Meet Student Needs ... 75
- Tips From the Top 80
- Voices From the Field 81
- Takeaway Tool Kit 83
- Wrap-Up 91

Chapter Four
Preparing and Implementing Collaborative IEPs 93
- Navigating the Complexities of IEPs 94
- Tips From the Top 109
- Voices From the Field 110
- Takeaway Tool Kit 111
- Wrap-Up 121

Chapter Five
Leveraging Digital Tools, Assistive Technology, and AI 123
- Technologies for Effective Communication 124
- Effective Technology Integration in Special Education 131
- Technologies to Support Documentation Storage and Project Management .. 132
- AI in Special Education 136
- Tips From the Top 141
- Voices From the Field 142
- Takeaway Tool Kit 144
- Wrap-Up 154

Chapter Six
Optimizing Workload Management and Performance Improvement ... 155
- Workload Management 156
- Strategies for Optimizing Workloads 159
- Supportive Performance Improvement With Collaborative Success Plans ... 169
- Tips From the Top 175

  Voices From the Field. 176
  Takeaway Tool Kit 177
  Wrap-Up 183

Epilogue 185
References and Resources 187
Index 197

About the Author

Breauna C. Wall, EdD, is a dedicated mother and an esteemed education professional with over a decade of experience as a teacher, leader, scholar, and practitioner. As the founder and CEO of CollaborativeEd Solutions, she champions equitable and collaborative education, with a focus on empowering inclusive practices. Dr. Wall empowers educators through transformative knowledge, training, and support. In addition to her role at CollaborativeEd Solutions, she is a Solution Tree author, teaching associate at Johns Hopkins University, clinical instructor at California State Polytechnic University, Pomona (Cal Poly Pomona), and co-host of *The Straight Ed Talks Podcast*, where she engages in critical conversations about inclusive and equitable education. These roles allow her to shape the minds of future educators and influence the field of education through thought leadership and collaboration.

Dr. Wall is a member of the American Educational Research Association. She has presented throughout the United States on topics such as empowering inclusive and equitable classrooms and championing collaborative approaches to special education. Dr. Wall's published work includes, but is not limited to, articles in the *Journal of Online Learning Research* and the Texas Association for the Gifted and Talented.

Dr. Wall holds a bachelor's degree in the sociology of law, criminology, and deviance from her home state's University of Minnesota, Twin Cities. She has a master of education degree in educational leadership and principalship from Northern Arizona University, a master of education degree in special education from Arizona State University, and a doctor of education degree from Johns Hopkins University specializing in the mind, brain, and teaching. Her lifelong passion for education is deeply rooted in her childhood, where she encountered both trauma and social injustices alongside profound joy, love, and laughter. These contrasting experiences have cultivated a resilient and optimistic drive within her, inspiring her to create positive transformations in education and beyond. Guided by the question "What are you doing for others?" and grounded in her Christian faith, Dr. Wall is committed to creating a meaningful, lasting impact in the educational community.

To learn more about Dr. Wall's work,
visit her website (www.collaborativeedsolutions.com).

To book Dr. Wall for professional development,
contact pd@SolutionTree.com.

Foreword

by Anthony Muhammad

Education has served as the platform for my life's mission: to make a positive impact on other people's lives. Life is a precarious journey. Everyone faces challenges and obstacles, and the ability to navigate those challenges can make the road of life more pleasant and rewarding. I always viewed my service as an educator as one that would help make students' life journeys a little easier through the lessons that I could teach them. Dr. Wall, through this book, has provided valuable lessons and tools for all of us to use in mitigating some of the challenges that our most vulnerable students, those with disabilities, face.

I entered kindergarten in 1974, before the iconic Individuals with Disabilities in Education Act (IDEA) was signed into law. As a young student, I was not keenly aware of physical and cognitive differences among my peers. All I knew was that we were energetic children who sought to be molded and shaped in ways that brought us joy and fulfillment. As kindergarten progressed, I noticed that some of my peers were separated and sometimes isolated from the rest of us. I noticed that books and assignments that I was given to take home for practice differed from what was given to some of my classmates. I noticed that the more these classmates were segregated and treated differently, the more they started to engage in disruptive behavior, displayed anger, and withdrew from engaging with the rest of us.

My teacher did not have a comprehensive and research-affirmed process to form an effective response to their needs. Instead, she doubled-down on their isolation, and as the year progressed, these students become more disruptive, angry, and disengaged. As I matriculated to the first grade the following year, two of my struggling classmates had to repeat kindergarten, and most of the other students struggled in first grade in the same ways they struggled the previous year.

My two classmates, both boys, who were retained in kindergarten were friends of mine from my neighborhood. I was aware that there were some slight differences in the words they used and their reactions to conflict as we played. But I never viewed them as deficient, just slightly different. I don't remember them being bullied or teased because of their differences. After repeating kindergarten, my two friends struggled in the primary grades, and by fourth grade, both were placed in a self-contained special education classroom.

We didn't know what their isolation meant educationally, but we knew that their classwork was less rigorous, their class had fewer than ten students, and they were systematically isolated from the rest of the school. The school system's attempt to "help" my kindergarten classmates only made their educational journey worse. They both began to get relentlessly teased, constantly engaged in arguments and fights, and as the rest of us seemed to academically and socially develop, they regressed. I never knew what their disabilities were. All I knew was that once they were diagnosed as "different," they started this tragic downward spiral from which they never recovered. As a child, I concluded that being placed in special education was a tragedy. I never witnessed anyone assigned for special education assistance thrive. It seemed as if my friends would have been better off never having been diagnosed with a disability.

That experience had a strong impact on me as a person, an educational professional, and ultimately as a father. When my oldest son was a toddler, we noticed that he had some delays in his speech and cognition. I prayed that this was something that would pass with time. My personal experience taught me that once a school system diagnoses a child as disabled, their doom is near! We worked relentlessly on my son's speech and language skills. We read to him day and night, and his speech and language patterns eventually improved. His handwriting was nearly illegible due to delayed motor skills, so we practiced with him daily. I even sent articles on fine motor skills and intelligence to his teachers so they would not prejudge his intelligence based upon his penmanship. We worked day and night to support him and keep him under the radar for being recommended for testing for a disability. Our efforts paid off. My son graduated from high school with a 3.0 grade point average and eventually attended college and earned a bachelor's degree. The sad moral of his story is that we worked relentlessly to support our son to keep him *out* of the special education system. We saw the system as detrimental to his chances of prospering in school. We did not view special education as a system that would provide him with the support he needed to thrive.

I wish that the educators who served my childhood friends and my son had access to this book. Dr. Wall has put together the most comprehensive framework that I've read to help any system that truly desires to see their students with disabilities thrive. She makes a moral, professional, and systemic case that is supported by research, experience, and practical tools. There is no reason that students should be destroyed by a system designed to help them or that parents should have to lobby to keep their children out of that system. Special education was meant to support and enhance the experience of students with intellectual and physical disabilities, but as Dr. Wall points out in this book, the current data does not validate that end. I implore you to read this book with an intention to apply its suggestions and recommendations and try to shift this to the norm. Her approach is comprehensive and practical. You cannot read this book and not be motivated to act. My greatest personal takeaway from this book is that pure intentions are noble, but effective action is better. All of us have our own personal stories about students with disabilities and the education system—let's strive to make the stories of the future joyful.

Introduction

When I say "special education," many people envision a classroom down the hall where students are sent for part of or the entire day or a virtual session with a small group of students. But special education is so much more than that. It exists wherever our students are—in gym class, on the playground, in science labs, reading clubs, before- and after-school programs, the lunchroom, the principal's or counselor's office, on the cheerleading team, and, of course, in our general classes. Special education is everywhere because our students are everywhere. In fact, among students with Individualized Education Programs (IEPs), 67 percent spend 80 percent or more of their school days in general education environments, 16 percent spend 40–79 percent of their days in general class environments, and 13 percent spend less than 40 percent of their time in general class environments (National Center for Education Statistics, 2024).

As school leaders, you are likely aware of the profound challenges that special education teachers face daily. The task of nurturing our most vulnerable students often comes with an overwhelming workload, sometimes insufficient support, and a constant battle against systemic inefficiencies. These educators are not just teachers—they are advocates, counselors, and steadfast champions for every student's right to quality education. The reality, however, is that the demands placed on them can lead to significant job dissatisfaction and burnout (Robinson, Bridges, Rollins, & Schumacker, 2019).

Special education teachers often leave the profession at higher rates than their general education counterparts due to these overwhelming workloads, insufficient resources, and administrative burdens (Hagaman & Casey, 2018). Research consistently highlights the link between teacher workload and job satisfaction. According to research, burnout is a leading cause of teachers leaving the profession (Emery & Vandenberg, 2010; Robinson et al., 2019; Shen et al., 2015). This trend is particularly alarming in special education, where the complexity and intensity of the workload can be even greater. Addressing these challenges is not just a matter of improving working conditions—it requires a comprehensive, supportive approach and a partnership with our educators to ensure the sustainability of our education system. Providing targeted professional learning experiences, fostering a supportive work environment, and leveraging data-driven decision making can significantly improve teacher job satisfaction and retention (Juniper Education, 2023; Robinson et al., 2019).

This book aims to equip you with the knowledge and tools to support your special education teachers effectively. School leaders, I am calling on you to pause, reflect, and plan for action to create sustainable, nurturing, and effective special education systems and ensure that all educators and students receive the support they need.

Why I Wrote This Book

As I was sitting in a coffee shop working on this book, I ran into the owner of a local business I support. He asked me how my book was coming along, as I had told him about it previously. He introduced me to his wife and asked me to remind him what my book is about. After I told them, his wife then shared that their son is in second grade and receives services to support his ADHD and speech-language uniqueness. They expressed their frustrations with the school system and how they felt like the system was failing their son.

His wife said that she understood teachers lack appropriate school support, pay, and sometimes training. Wow! Two parents testifying to the sad realities many teachers face! They even went on to describe how she could tell that their son's current teacher is burnt out and that a burdensome teacher shortage persists. As parents, they described feeling at a loss, and they wondered if they should withdraw their son from his current school and try another school. This encounter was a powerful reminder of the urgency of this book—a walking testimony describing the need for effective strategies and support in special education.

Special education is a field that has the potential to empower students and transform lives. Over the past decade working in special education, I have experienced myriad emotions: I've been inspired, let down, filled with joy, frustrated, and fortified. This book aims to support school leaders in their mission to improve and enhance special education. My goal is to provide knowledge and tools that help you retain special education teachers, improve their job satisfaction, ensure successful programs, and, ultimately, make a positive impact on students.

There are numerous factors that impact teacher retention, and one of the biggest is the need for greater compensation. Compensation is not a focus in this book, but I'd be remiss if I didn't highlight the importance of urgently addressing compensation. While the issue of teacher salaries is critical and warrants ongoing attention, this book focuses on strategies and tools that school leaders can leverage to improve job satisfaction and retention within the scope of their immediate influence. Please don't mistake the omission of direct discussion of teachers' salaries throughout this book as an indication that it's not important, because it is. Special education teachers need to be paid fairly as a baseline for job satisfaction and retention. My greatest hope for this book is for you to find it inspiring, resourceful, and empowering, encouraging you to evolve your thinking and processes to improve teacher retention, job satisfaction, and program success in special education.

While this book is primarily designed for those not exclusively serving special education schools, special day programs, or self-contained learning environments, there are undoubtedly elements within these pages that will resonate and be beneficial across various educational contexts. The insights shared are grounded in both research and practical experiences, focusing on inclusive settings where students in special education programs integrate with general education and other specialized educational models.

I hope you will agree that this book addresses the dynamics of both traditional and online K–12 school environments. I've been fortunate to serve as a practitioner in brick-and-mortar, hybrid, and online schools throughout my career, and I have intentionally kept you all in mind throughout my writing process. In education, much of the available literature tends to focus on conventional classroom settings, and at times overlooks the unique challenges and opportunities inherent in online and hybrid learning. This book aims to bridge that gap and present solutions for all learning formats.

What's in This Book

This book is crafted for K–12 school leaders in brick-and-mortar, hybrid, and online schools. It discusses the nuances and strategies essential for thriving in these diverse educational environments and aims to equip you with the knowledge and practical strategies necessary to honor and support your teachers while fulfilling your duty of managing successful special education programs.

By *leaders*, I am referring to anyone in a position of leadership within a school setting—not just administrators. This includes department chairs, instructional coaches, team leads, and any educator who has a role in guiding colleagues, shaping policies, or influencing the culture of their school. Leadership in education comes in many forms, and this book is for all who take on the responsibility of making a positive impact on teachers and students alike.

Whether you are navigating the complexities of integrating special education into an inclusive school environment or adapting to the demands of online education, this book aims to provide you with valuable insights and actionable strategies to enhance your practice and positively support your special educators, programs, and, ultimately, students.

- Chapter 1 provides practical strategies for building a supportive culture through mentorship and discusses the critical importance of connection.
- Chapter 2 addresses the critical role of school leaders in fostering an environment that supports continuous professional learning for special education and partner teachers.
- Chapter 3 explores the transformative power of collective pedagogy in special education and highlights strategies for effective co-teaching and co-planning to support teacher and student success.
- Chapter 4 addresses the importance of collaborative IEP preparation and implementation and emphasizes the roles of all team members in crafting and executing effective IEPs.
- Chapter 5 shows how school leaders can champion digital literacy and integrate technology to support teachers, professional work habits, and student learning outcomes.
- Chapter 6 presents innovative ways school leaders can optimize special educators' workloads for efficiency and transform traditional

performance improvement methods into supportive, growth-focused practices.

Each chapter includes recurring features designed to provide practical tools and thought-provoking reflections.

Tips From the Top

These sections offer actionable, high-level guidance for school leaders to address key challenges discussed in the chapter. Unlike the broader advice woven throughout the chapter, these tips focus on succinct, targeted strategies that leaders can implement immediately to enhance communication, foster collaboration, and drive impactful change within their schools.

Voices From the Field

The Voices From the Field sections feature stories shared by teachers and administrators who have navigated the complex and rewarding world of teaching and mentoring. These accounts are more than just examples—they are living testaments to the resilience, creativity, and dedication of those working to make a difference in education. These sections provide invaluable insights drawn from real challenges and triumphs.

Takeaway Tool Kit

The Takeaway Tool Kit provides ready-to-use resources and tools that school leaders can apply directly to their work. These might include checklists, templates, conversation starters, or actionable steps tailored to the chapter's focus. The Tool Kit section is designed to bridge theory and practice, aiming to ensure that concepts are not just understood but effectively applied.

Wrap-Up

Each chapter concludes with a Wrap-Up section, which offers a reflective summary of the key ideas and strategies presented. It encourages leaders to think deeply about their own practices and how they can create a supportive and thriving environment for educators and students. The Wrap-Up section ties together the chapter's themes and motivates readers to take intentional steps toward positive change.

I hope this book's practical strategies and actionable insights empower school leaders of all sorts—curriculum directors, instructional coaches, principals, assistant principals, lead teachers, and so on—to create supportive, effective, and inclusive educational environments. I hope you find something within these pages that inspires you and provides the resources you need to make a meaningful difference in the world of special education.

Chapter One

Retaining Special Educators Through Systems of Support

Connections matter. When I reflect on my most valuable moments as a practitioner, they involve other people: debriefing after a challenging day, sharing laughter with colleagues and students' parents, being shoulder partners during an all-day professional development session, planning an upcoming school event, and brainstorming ways to solve the ongoing challenges we face in the field. There aren't enough words in a dictionary to describe the immeasurable transformation that can blossom through human connection.

If someone told you, a school leader, that taking time to foster meaningful connections with your staff could be life-changing, would you consider this information vitally important and apply it to practice? I think of *connection* as the act of linking two or more people together; facilitating communication, interaction, or unity among them; and emphasizing the importance of relationships in achieving shared understanding, goals, and a sense of belonging and community.

In the introduction to the book *Relationship-Rich Education: How Human Connections Drive Success in College* by Peter Felten and Leo M. Lambert (2020), Randy Bass of Georgetown University defines *human connection* as "the basis upon which learning takes place. Relationships are essential because there is no learning without relationships" (p. 1). Felten and Lambert (2020) then present a compelling case for the essential role that deep and sustained connections play among staff, faculty, and mentors. All educational institutions can cultivate meaningful relationships that ultimately impact the overall success of the community.

Stanford University's Center for Compassion and Altruism Research and Education highlights the critical importance of social connectedness for health (Seppala, 2014). The absence of social connections poses a greater risk to health than obesity, smoking, and high blood pressure, which emphasizes the profound impact of social ties on physical and mental well-being (Seppala, 2014).

Priya J. Wickramaratne and her colleagues (2022), in a review of research studies from 2015 to 2021, find that social support and strong social networks significantly protect against depressive symptoms, while loneliness and limited social networks increase the risk of depression and anxiety. Though not specific to schools, their research underscores the importance of fostering connections in social environments like educational institutions. For school leaders, this means prioritizing opportunities for staff to build meaningful relationships, such as through mentorship programs or team-building initiatives. By strengthening social bonds, leaders can enhance staff well-being and create a more resilient school community.

Our overall health and well-being impact how we function within the school system. We know this to be true for our students, and it's certainly true for our staff. By developing and maintaining connections in your school community, you are creating a foundation that contributes to a healthier, more unified and resilient educational community.

This chapter appears first in this book to emphasize the importance of support and set a foundation of connection and mentorship as central to this important work we do. Developing and fostering connections with people we serve is an underused key to transforming school culture and achieving success as leaders. This has the power to positively contribute to teacher retention and program success! I am a living testament to the positive effects of intentionally fostering personal and professional connections in our schools and within our communities. I have thrived as an educator through healthy, positive, and meaningful connections with my supervisors and supervisees, colleagues, community partners, parents, and students. I have witnessed firsthand the detrimental impact of a school culture where leaders either remain unaware of or underestimate the transformative power of building meaningful connections, and where teachers lack mentorship and leaders lack connections to the people they intend to lead.

This chapter is designed to highlight the transformative power of fostering strong, meaningful relationships among your staff that have the potential to positively contribute to your entire school community. Through discussions on mentorship and how to effectively foster meaningful connections, we will explore practical strategies and insights that can contribute to your teachers' sense of belonging in your school community, with a goal of ultimately impacting their success and desire to continue serving in our field. By prioritizing and cultivating these essential connections, we open doors to a more unified, resilient, and successful educational community. Let's lay the groundwork for a culture that cherishes and thrives on deep, sustained human connections.

Improving Relationships and Culture With Mentorship

In the United States, a substantial number of schools have implemented mentorship or induction programs for new teachers. A report by the National Center for Education Statistics (2020) indicates that during the 2017–2018 school year, 79 percent of new teachers worked closely with a mentor teacher. This widespread adoption emphasizes the recognized importance of mentorship in the educational landscape (National Center for Education Statistics, 2020).

Moreover, mentorship has been found to significantly impact student achievement. Research consistently shows that mentorship programs designed to provide subject-specific guidance and induction support can dramatically improve student outcomes (Will, 2017). This emphasizes the dual benefit of mentorship not only in supporting teacher retention but also in positively influencing classroom performance and student success.

Structure of Mentorship Programs

The design of mentorship programs can differ based on school or district policies, school resources, and specific objectives. Common elements include the following.

- **Mentor assignment:** Pairing novice teachers with experienced educators who provide guidance, support, and feedback. These relationships create opportunities for new teachers to learn from experienced professionals and receive targeted advice tailored to their specific challenges (Teach for America, n.d.).

- **Professional development:** Offering workshops, training sessions, and collaborative planning opportunities to enhance teaching skills. Programs that emphasize professional growth foster better instructional practices and create pathways for continuous improvement (Hightower, Wiens, & Guzman, 2021).

- **Observation and feedback:** Facilitating classroom observations, followed by constructive feedback to promote reflective practice. Effective mentorship programs integrate opportunities for new teachers to receive actionable feedback that helps refine their teaching methods (Frasier, 2022).

- **Emotional support:** Creating a supportive environment where teachers, especially new teachers, can discuss challenges and successes. Emotional support plays a critical role in fostering teacher confidence and addressing burnout, ensuring that mentees feel valued and connected to their school community (Hanover Research, 2018).

Despite the prevalence of these programs, their effectiveness can be influenced by many factors, such as the quality of mentor-mentee matching, the frequency and depth of interactions, and the availability of resources. Research suggests that well-structured programs focusing on professional development and collaboration are more successful in retaining beginning teachers (Hightower et al., 2021).

While many schools have mentorship programs, not all are equally effective. Challenges include insufficient training for mentors, lack of time for meaningful interactions, and inadequate funding. Additionally, teachers in low-income schools and STEM educators are less likely to report receiving high-quality mentoring and induction supports, which indicates disparities in program implementation (Hanover Research, 2018). Furthermore, some programs lack a clear framework for success, which diminishes their ability to address the specific needs of new teachers (Hightower et al., 2021).

Implications for Special Education

The need for effective mentorship is even more pronounced due to the unique challenges special education teachers face. Tailoring mentorship programs to address these specific needs—such as managing diverse learner needs, adhering to legal requirements, and implementing specialized instructional strategies—is crucial. Mentorship programs that incorporate high-leverage practices (HLPs) offer a structured framework that enhances teaching efficacy and promotes retention among special education teachers (Hightower et al., 2021). We'll talk more about HLPs later in this section.

Understanding the current landscape of mentorship programs, including their prevalence, structure, and limitations, provides a foundation for developing more effective strategies tailored to the needs of special education professionals. This awareness sets the stage for the subsequent how-to guide and program design worksheet, which aim to assist in establishing comprehensive mentorship frameworks that contribute significantly to the success of special education programs.

Mentorship in special education transcends conventional support, and it can be a game changer in the world of teaching diverse learners. Thomas M. Smith and Richard M. Ingersoll (2004) lay the foundational understanding of the impact of mentorship, highlighting how subject-specific guidance and collective induction efforts can significantly reduce teacher turnover. With new-teacher attrition rates still alarming, mentoring can serve as a conduit of emotional and professional support (Crawford & Toledo, 2023).

Building on this insight, researchers Roddy J. Theobald, Dan D. Goldhaber, Natsumi Naito, and Marcy L. Stein (2021) further spotlight the critical role of mentorship in special education, revealing that candidates who receive mentorship from special education–certified teachers are more likely to stay in their roles. This combined perspective not only highlights the importance of mentorship for professional and personal growth but emphasizes its power in retaining teachers within the special education field, nurturing a sense of resilience and belonging.

Mentorship programs should be designed to offer a blend of professional guidance, emotional support, and practical teaching strategies tailored to the unique challenges of special education. Continuous mentorship allows leaders to provide a pathway of personalized guidance that meets the specific needs of each staff member, whether they are just beginning their career, aiming to enhance their teaching methods, or leading others toward educational excellence.

In crafting mentorship programs that resonate with the unique demands of special education, incorporating HLPs is paramount. *HLPs* are twenty-two core practices identified by the Council for Exceptional Children that encompass key areas such as collaboration, assessment, and instruction. These practices provide a structured framework for mentoring and professional development. Bonnie Billingsley, Elizabeth Bettini, and Nathan D. Jones (2019) emphasize the importance of aligning mentorship programs with HLPs to address the complex, often ambiguous roles of special education teachers.

A mentorship program grounded in HLPs might focus on guiding new educators through collaborative strategies like co-teaching (HLP 1) or effective meetings with IEP team members (HLP 2), ensuring consistent and impactful teacher-student interactions. By embedding HLPs into mentorship, we can send clear messages about instructional expectations, improve teaching efficacy, and foster teacher retention—all critical for the success of special education programs. Smith and Ingersoll (2004) reinforce this approach, illustrating that structured mentorship, combined with supportive induction activities, nurtures an ecosystem where educators thrive. Programs that emphasize reflective practice, collaborative planning, and specialized instructional strategies can significantly elevate the mentor-mentee dynamic, setting the stage for sustained professional development and teacher retention.

In this context, *reflective practice* refers to teachers systematically reflecting on their pedagogy, student interactions, and lived experiences and leveraging the insights they gain to improve their practices. Mentors can play a crucial role in guiding and modeling this practice for their mentees. Mentors should encourage self-assessment, provide constructive feedback, and foster a mindset of continuous improvement. Such reflective practices can lead to personal and professional development and ultimately enhance the quality of education for our students.

Collaborative planning is another critical aspect of mentorship where mentors and mentees work together to leverage data and design and implement effective instructional plans. This collaborative space creates an environment conducive to sharing ideas, strategies, and resources. Through collaborative planning, mentors can model effective pedagogy and help mentees develop their knowledge and skills in creating inclusive and engaging lesson plans. This has the potential to enhance instructional practices and foster a sense of community and shared purpose among educators.

Specially designed instruction, also referred to as *specialized instruction*, is essential to meeting the needs of diverse learners. The federal Individuals with Disabilities Education Act (2004) defines specially designed instruction as follows:

> Specially designed instruction means adapting, as appropriate to the needs of an eligible child under this part, the content, methodology, or delivery of instruction—
>> (i) To address the unique needs of the child that result from the child's disability; and
>> (ii) To ensure access of the child to the general curriculum, so that the child can meet the educational standards within the jurisdiction of the public agency that apply to all children.

Tailoring instructional strategies can help us break down barriers that hinder our students' learning and accessibility. According to Christina Bain, Jeff Young, and Deborah Kuster (2017), mentors can model a variety of instructional strategies, granting the mentee opportunities to observe and practice under trusted guidance, leading to the development of self-efficacy and confidence in implementing specialized instructional practices. Mentees should receive advice on how to adapt strategies to different class situations, students, and program plans. Bain and colleagues (2017) refer to advancement as the *mentor approach*, which encourages mentees to try out instructional strategies while the mentor gives advice along the way.

LaRon A. Scott and colleagues (2022) emphasize the transformative potential of mentorship in retaining special education teachers. The study investigates factors associated with special education teachers' persistence in their careers using Albert Bandura's (1977) social cognitive theory and asserts mentorship programs contribute directly to enhancing teacher efficacy by providing the tools, confidence, and support needed for success (Scott et al., 2022). This, in turn, boosts job satisfaction and commitment to the field, which are crucial for retaining teachers. Developing mentorship programs that resonate with the unique needs of special education involves acknowledging and addressing several key areas.

- **Empowering teachers through targeted support:** Mentorship tailored to the unique demands of special education empowers teachers with the confidence and competence needed to navigate their challenging roles. Special educators often grapple with high caseloads, diverse student needs, limited administrative guidance, and intricate legal requirements. A mentor, especially one with specialized experience, provides not just advice but also emotional support, practical strategies, and an understanding ear. This targeted support is instrumental in transforming potential overwhelm into manageable challenges, enabling teachers to thrive in their roles.

- **Fostering a culture of continuous learning:** The dynamic nature of special education, with its evolving best practices and legislative changes, demands ongoing professional development. Mentorship creates a structured pathway for continuous learning, where mentees can regularly update their skills and knowledge in a supportive environment. This culture of growth not only benefits the individual teachers but also enriches the learning experiences of their students, leading to improved outcomes and program success.

- **Creating a sense of community and belonging:** Special education can feel isolating, with teachers sometimes working apart from their general education colleagues. Effective mentorship programs can help bridge this gap, fostering a strong sense of community and belonging among special education staff. This collegial network can reduce feelings of isolation and encourage the sharing of resources, strategies, and successes. A connected and supported teacher is more likely to remain in their position, contributing to higher retention rates.

- **Addressing the unique challenges of special education:** The mentor-mentee relationship offers a safe space to address the specific challenges inherent to special education. From supporting diverse behaviors to adapting curriculum for diverse learners, mentors can guide new teachers through these hurdles with practical advice and empathy. By demystifying these challenges, mentorship helps retain teachers who might otherwise leave the profession due to stress or burnout.

- **Enhancing teacher efficacy and job satisfaction:** It's well documented that a teacher's belief in their ability to impact student learning—known as *self-efficacy*—plays a critical role in their job satisfaction and retention (Bandura, 1977). This connection highlights the importance of fostering environments where teachers feel competent and capable. Self-efficacy not only directly enhances job satisfaction but enriches the school climate, which in turn contributes to teacher retention (Ortan, Simut, & Simut, 2021).

Structured mentorship programs can truly be a powerful strategy to enhance teacher efficacy. These programs offer new educators essential tools, resources, and support, increasing their confidence and effectiveness in the classroom. The resulting sense of achievement and professional fulfillment is vital for sustaining teachers' motivation and commitment to their roles. As demonstrated in the research, such initiatives lead to a positive work environment where both teachers and students thrive, significantly lowering teacher turnover and emotional exhaustion (Ortan et al., 2021). By investing in mentorship programs, we can create a supportive atmosphere that not only boosts teacher efficacy but also anchors them more deeply in their educational communities.

We will now transition into hands-on, practical tools and strategies designed to help you build, refine, and sustain effective mentorship programs in support of special education. The sections that follow break down critical components of mentorship into actionable steps, guiding you through key elements such as mentor-mentee matching, mentor training, feedback mechanisms, and technology integration. These practical tools have theoretical underpinnings and are designed to bridge the gap between theory and practice, offering you actionable, ready-to-implement strategies.

The aim is to equip you with resources like questionnaires, checklists, and feedback surveys, as well as provide you with insights into how to implement them effectively. From aligning mentors and mentees thoughtfully to recognizing and rewarding the efforts of your staff, these sections are built to help you create mentorship programs that support teacher growth, enhance student outcomes, and foster a culture of collaboration and retention.

As you move into these detailed sections, keep in mind that each step is part of a larger goal: to empower educators and build a supportive environment where teachers and students can thrive. Let's dive in and explore how you can bring these ideas to life, starting with the foundational element of mentor and mentee matching.

Mentor and Mentee Matching

As a first step, leaders must develop a systematic approach to pair mentors with mentees based on teaching styles, personality compatibility, and professional goals. Effective mentor-mentee matches require intentional planning to ensure that both parties feel aligned and supported. The following action steps can guide you in achieving this objective.

1. Develop a questionnaire to capture the preferences, strengths, and areas for development of both potential mentors and mentees.
2. Use a matching algorithm or committee to pair individuals based on their questionnaire responses, ensuring alignment in educational philosophies and personalities.
3. Conduct initial meet-and-greet sessions to confirm compatibility and allow for rematching if necessary.

Mentoring is a powerful way to communicate instructional expectations and enhance teacher effectiveness (Billingsley et al., 2019). Structured mentoring enables new teachers to apply complex practices they've studied, bridging the gap between theory and practice in the hustle of daily teaching. According to Billingsley and colleagues (2019), this structured approach is essential in equipping new teachers with the tools they need to start strong and reduce uncertainties in their roles, particularly in special education. By embracing these mentoring principles, you can foster a culture of continuous learning and improvement, a cornerstone of long-term success in educational programs.

Mentor-Mentee Pairing Questionnaire

To facilitate effective matching, a well-designed questionnaire can serve as a critical tool for gathering the necessary information about mentors and mentees. The "Mentor-Mentee Pairing Questionnaire" (figure 1.1) provides a structured way to identify preferences, strengths, and areas for development, ensuring that pairings are intentional and impactful. By incorporating questions about teaching philosophy, communication style, and availability, this tool aims to support you in collecting information that you can leverage to make informed decisions that align mentor and mentee needs with the program's goals. Following is a sample of what this questionnaire could look like in practice. I encourage you to consider the unique needs of your online, hybrid, or brick-and-mortar school and amend where necessary.

Mentor-Mentee Pairing Questionnaire

Name: *Hector G.*

Role (Mentor or Mentee): *Mentee*

Grade Level and Subject Area: *Grade 5 mathematics*

Years of Teaching Experience: *2*

Section 1: Preferences and Strengths

1. Teaching Philosophy
   How would you describe your teaching philosophy?
   I believe in a student-centered approach that emphasizes hands-on learning and critical thinking.
2. Preferred Communication Style
   How do you prefer to communicate (email, in-person meetings, phone calls)?
   I prefer in-person meetings supplemented by regular emails.
3. Strengths
   What do you consider your greatest strengths as an educator?
   Classroom management, curriculum development, and fostering student engagement
4. Areas for Development
   In which areas would you like to further develop your skills?
   Integrating technology into the classroom and differentiated instruction
5. Preferred Mentor or Mentee Characteristics
   What qualities are you looking for in a mentor or mentee?
   I am looking for a mentor who is approachable, has experience with diverse student populations, and is innovative in their teaching methods.

Section 2: Educational Background and Experience

6. Educational Background
   Please summarize your educational background and any relevant certifications.
   Bachelor's in elementary education, master's in special education, certified in TESOL
7. Professional Experience
   Briefly describe your teaching experience and any leadership roles you have held.
   I have been teaching fifth grade for two years.

Section 3: Availability and Commitment

8. Availability
   How often are you available to meet with your mentor or mentee with respect to your current schedule?
   I am available for biweekly meetings and can communicate via email throughout the week.
9. Commitment
   Are you willing to commit to a mentorship program for a full academic year?
   Yes

continued >

Figure 1.1: Mentor-mentee pairing questionnaire example.

> **Section 4: Additional Information**
> 10. Strategies for Mentor-Mentee Relationships
>   What do you believe are effective strategies for fostering an effective mentor-mentee relationship?
>   *Effective strategies include setting clear expectations from the start, establishing open and honest communication, providing regular and constructive feedback, creating a supportive environment where the mentee feels comfortable sharing challenges, and celebrating successes together.*
> 11. Additional Details
>   Please share any other information that you think would be helpful in pairing you with a mentor or mentee.
>   *I have a background in art education and would love to incorporate more creative projects into my teaching.*

Visit **go.SolutionTree.com/specialneeds** for a free reproducible version of this figure.

Mentor Training

Up next, mentor training! Training and development should aim to equip mentors with the critical skills for effective mentorship, focusing on communication, feedback, and adult learning strategies. The following are actions you can take to meet this objective.

- Invite experts in adult education and mentorship to facilitate workshops.
- Create a resource hub with access to articles, videos, and case studies on successful mentorship practices.
- Identify key areas of mentorship skill development and organize comprehensive training sessions. Here are key skills you might consider.
  - **Effective communication:** Train mentors in active listening, open questioning, and clear, constructive dialogue. Effective communication is foundational to successful mentoring relationships, as it builds trust and ensures clear understanding between mentors and mentees (Eby, Allen, Evans, Ng, & DuBois, 2008).
  - **Feedback:** Develop mentors' abilities to give timely, specific, and constructive feedback that encourages reflection and growth. Research underscores the critical role of feedback in enhancing professional performance and development (Hattie & Timperley, 2007).

- **Adult learning strategies:** Equip mentors with strategies tailored to adult learning, such as self-directed learning and experiential techniques. Adult learners benefit from practical, relevant, and collaborative learning experiences that apply directly to their work or personal goals (Cox, 2015; Cranton & Taylor, 2012).
- **Cultural competence:** Training in cultural competence is essential, as mentors often work with mentees from diverse backgrounds. This training should cover understanding different cultural perspectives and applying this understanding to enhance mentoring relationships (Gay, 2018).
- **Emotional intelligence:** Incorporate training that enhances mentors' emotional intelligence, which is crucial for managing and nurturing professional relationships effectively. Skills such as empathy, self-regulation, and social fluency are particularly valuable (Zeidner et al., 2009).

Feedback Mechanisms

Establish structured feedback channels for continuous program evaluation and improvement. The following are actions you can take to meet this objective.

- Implement at least one quarterly check-in meeting between mentors and mentees to discuss progress and challenges.
- Introduce anonymous online surveys for gathering feedback from all program participants.
- Review feedback regularly to identify areas for improvement and adjust program elements as needed.

To get you started, figure 1.2 (page 20) is an example of a feedback survey designed specifically for mentorship programs. I created this tool with the intention of helping you gather honest input from mentors and mentees about their experiences, which will provide you with insight into what's working and where there's room for improvement. The survey is simple to implement, and you can customize it to fit the unique needs of your school. Regularly collecting feedback like this ensures your program stays aligned with its goals and continues to meet the needs of everyone involved.

Mentorship Program Feedback Survey

Your feedback is crucial for us to understand the effectiveness of our mentorship program and to make necessary improvements. Please answer the following questions honestly. Your responses will remain completely anonymous.

Section 1: General Information

1. What is your role?
   - ☐ Mentor
   - ☑ Mentee

Section 2: Program Satisfaction

2. How satisfied are you with the mentorship program overall?
   - ☐ Very satisfied
   - ☑ Satisfied
   - ☐ Neutral
   - ☐ Dissatisfied
   - ☐ Very dissatisfied

3. To what extent has the mentorship program met your initial expectations?
   - ☑ Exceeded expectations
   - ☐ Met expectations
   - ☐ Somewhat met expectations
   - ☐ Did not meet expectations
   - ☐ Significantly did not meet expectations

Section 3: Specific Experiences

4. How well does the program support your professional development needs?
   - ☐ Very well
   - ☑ Well
   - ☐ Adequately
   - ☐ Poorly
   - ☐ Very poorly

5. How effective is the communication between you and your mentor or mentee?
   - ☐ Very effective
   - ☐ Effective
   - ☑ Moderately effective
   - ☐ Ineffective
   - ☐ Very ineffective

6. How valuable is the feedback you receive from your mentor or mentee?
   - ☐ Extremely valuable
   - ☑ Very valuable
   - ☐ Moderately valuable
   - ☐ Slightly valuable
   - ☐ Not at all valuable

Section 4: Program Implementation

7. How frequently do you meet with your mentor or mentee?
   - ☐ More than once a week
   - ☐ Weekly
   - ☐ Biweekly
   - ☑ Monthly
   - ☐ Less than once a month

> 8. Are the resources and tools provided for the mentorship effective in aiding your mentoring relationship?
>   ☐ Extremely effective
>   ☐ Very effective
>   ☒ Moderately effective
>   ☐ Slightly effective
>   ☐ Not at all effective
> 9. How satisfied are you with the school administration's support of the mentorship program?
>   ☒ Very satisfied
>   ☐ Satisfied
>   ☐ Neutral
>   ☐ Dissatisfied
>   ☐ Very dissatisfied
> 10. What has been the most beneficial aspect of the mentorship program?
>   *The texts and tools I was provided; having someone to reach out to if I had an issue*
> 11. What improvements would you suggest for the mentorship program?
>   *More communication would be really appreciated, and more frequent meetings. It was helpful, but I wish we had met more often after the first weeks of the school year.*

Figure 1.2: Anonymous mentorship program feedback survey example.

*Visit **go.SolutionTree.com/specialneeds** for a free reproducible version of this figure.*

Technology Integration

Technology can be leveraged to enhance mentorship experience and accessibility. The following are actions you can take to meet this objective.

- Identify and deploy digital platforms that facilitate seamless communication and resource sharing between mentors and mentees. Identifying and deploying digital tools can be quite an adventure! Consider partnering with colleagues interested in helping you explore digital platforms.
- Provide training on how to use these platforms effectively.
- Explore virtual reality or augmented reality tools for simulating classroom scenarios and sharing best practices.

Recognition and Incentives for Participation

Motivate and acknowledge the contributions of mentors through recognition and incentives. The following are actions you can take to meet this objective.

- Develop a recognition program that includes certificates, awards, or public acknowledgments.
- Offer professional development credits for participation in the mentorship program.
- Plan an annual event to celebrate the achievements of mentorship pairs.

Sustainability Planning

Ensuring the long-term success and impact of the mentorship program can be achieved by planning for sustainability. The following are actions you can take to meet this objective.

- Engage school leadership and stakeholders in discussions about the value and impact of the mentorship program.
- Align the program with the school's broader strategic goals to secure ongoing support.
- Explore grants and external funding opportunities to enhance program offerings.

Now that we've explored the foundational components of mentorship programs—mentor-mentee matching, mentor training, feedback mechanisms, technology integration, recognition and incentives, and sustainability planning—it's time to build on these elements to create a comprehensive mentorship initiative. The strategies and tools shared in the previous section are integral to fostering effective mentorship relationships and laying the groundwork for a supportive school culture. Next, we'll focus on designing a structured program that brings these pieces together, ensuring alignment with your school's goals and the unique needs of your team. Let's move into the program design phase, where you'll begin crafting a framework for a mentorship initiative that supports teacher growth, fosters collaboration, and ultimately enhances student outcomes.

In the next section, you'll find a completed example of a program design worksheet to guide your planning process. This tool will help you translate the concepts and strategies we've discussed into a practical plan tailored to your school's needs.

Program Design

It's time to roll up our sleeves and put these insights into action. In figure 1.3 (page 24), you'll find a completed example of a program design worksheet, which is intended to jump-start your thinking and planning process. The program design worksheet is a practical tool for you to start crafting your own mentorship programs. This worksheet is your canvas to outline how you'll bring mentorship magic into your school, catering to the unique needs of your team and, ultimately, your students. Think of it as translating our conversation into a concrete plan that will breathe life into your mentorship initiatives. Ready to dive in? Let's make mentorship a vibrant reality in your educational community.

While this example outlines a comprehensive approach to building a mentorship program tailored for special education, it's crucial to adapt these suggestions to fit the specific contexts and unique challenges of your school. Use this as a foundation to inspire and inform your customized plan, ensuring it aligns seamlessly with your school's goals, culture, and the specific needs of your educators and students. As you proceed, remember the most effective programs are those that are thoughtfully aligned with local conditions and continuously refined based on participant feedback and evolving educational priorities.

While mentorship programs provide structured support and guidance, their success—and the success of any school initiative—depends on the connections they foster. Mentorship is, at its core, a relationship built on trust, shared understanding, and collaboration. These same elements are the lifeblood of a thriving school community, where meaningful connections among staff, students, and families create the foundation for resilience and success.

This chapter began by emphasizing the transformative power of connections, and it's clear that these bonds extend far beyond the mentorship pair. Whether it's through open dialogue, empathetic communication, or shared experiences, connections hold a school together. As we transition from mentorship to the broader role of connection, we'll explore how fostering relationships at every level in your school can drive positive outcomes for both staff and students. Connection is more than a strategy—it's the heartbeat of a supportive and successful educational community.

Program Goals	Launch a mentorship program or enhance current mentorship program to support teachers and improve job satisfaction and retention. Support new hires during their first three years to help them acclimate to and thrive in their roles. Identify experienced educators who demonstrate leadership qualities and a commitment to professional growth to serve as mentors.
Target Audience	New special education teachers and experienced educators interested in becoming mentors
Mentor Selection Criteria	**Minimum Requirements:** At least three years of teaching experience Credentialed Demonstrated leadership qualities and commitment to professional development **Goals:** Identify and select mentors with strong teaching expertise and leadership potential. Ensure mentors hold the necessary qualifications to maintain high standards of mentorship. Prioritize mentors who show enthusiasm for sharing knowledge and supporting new teachers.
Mentee Selection Criteria	**Focus Areas:** New teachers in their first three years Teachers seeking specific professional development in areas like behavioral management or differentiated instruction **Goals:** Tailor mentorship support to address the unique needs of each mentee. Foster professional growth and confidence in mentees through targeted guidance.
Mentor-Mentee Matching	**Process:** Use a structured questionnaire to capture teaching philosophies, personality traits, and professional aspirations. Pair mentors and mentees through an algorithm or committee based on their questionnaire responses. Conduct initial meet-and-greet sessions to confirm compatibility and allow for rematching if necessary. **Goals:** Facilitate mentor-mentee pairings that foster trust and collaboration. Ensure alignment in educational philosophies, communication preferences, and personal goals.

Training and Professional Development	**Workshops and Embedded Support:** Schedule multiple workshops at the start of the year, middle of the year, and end of the year. Cover topics such as adaptive communication strategies, feedback delivery, and adult learning principles. Incorporate team-building exercises to strengthen mentor-mentee relationships. **Professional Networks and Collaboration:** Organize monthly mentorship meetups to foster ongoing community and learning. Facilitate participation in annual special education conferences for broader exposure to practices and innovations. Support teacher-led professional learning workshops to enhance collaboration and share best practices. **Innovative Teaching Strategies:** Encourage mentors to share successful strategies and case studies. Host guided discussion sessions to adapt these strategies for different contexts. Create a virtual resource library to house tools, strategies, and professional development materials. **Emotional Support and Resilience Building:** Conduct regular resilience-building workshops focused on stress management. Establish peer support groups for ongoing emotional and professional guidance. Ensure access to counseling services for educators in need of additional support.
Technology Integration	**Strategies:** Leverage platforms like Microsoft Teams and Google Classroom for communication and resource sharing. Explore virtual reality tools for classroom simulation and collaborative learning. Provide training sessions on using these tools effectively. **Goals:** Streamline communication between mentors and mentees. Foster innovative teaching practices through accessible technology. Enhance engagement with immersive and interactive digital tools.

continued >

Figure 1.3: Mentorship program design worksheet example.

Recognition and Incentives	**Acknowledgment Strategies:** Award certificates of completion to mentors and mentees. Offer continuing education credits to encourage participation in professional development. Recognize outstanding participants in school newsletters and public events. **Goals:** Motivate mentors and mentees to actively engage in the program. Celebrate achievements to reinforce a culture of support and collaboration.
Implementation Timeline	**Phases:** Program Launch: Begin with a comprehensive introduction and orientation at the start of the academic year. Midyear Review: Conduct progress assessments and make necessary adjustments. End-of-Year Evaluation: Gather feedback to inform future improvements. **Goals:** Ensure a seamless rollout of the mentorship program. Maintain alignment with program goals through regular check-ins and adjustments.
Resources Needed	Budget allocation for training sessions, mentor compensation, and workshops Necessary technology tools for communication, resource sharing, and professional development Compensation for mentors, expert speakers, and facilitators to ensure high-quality training experiences
Evaluation and Feedback Mechanisms	**Process:** Conduct biannual surveys to gather feedback from participants. Hold annual review meetings with stakeholders to discuss progress and areas for improvement. Use performance data to evaluate the program's impact on teacher retention and professional growth. **Goals:** Ensure continuous improvement through structured feedback channels. Align program adjustments with the needs and experiences of participants.
Next Steps	Finalize mentor and mentee applications by the end of next month. Arrange logistics for initial training sessions, ensuring all materials and preparations are complete.

Visit **go.SolutionTree.com/specialneeds** *for a free reproducible version of this figure.*

Understanding the Power of Connections

At the heart of every thriving educational community lies the strength of its connections. Human connection is not just a nicety—it's a necessity. The relationships we build with our staff, students, and families create the foundation for everything we aim to accomplish. When leaders intentionally foster meaningful connections, they empower educators to feel supported, valued, and heard. These connections are the invisible threads that weave trust, collaboration, and resilience into the fabric of a school's culture.

For special education, the power of connections is crucial. The unique challenges special educators face—from managing diverse student needs to navigating extensive administrative demands—can often lead to feelings of isolation. By cultivating authentic relationships and prioritizing connection, school leaders can provide the support educators need to thrive. Whether it's through mentorship programs, team-building activities, or simply taking the time to listen, every effort to strengthen relationships contributes to a healthier, more unified school community.

In this section, we'll explore the role of effective communication in strengthening these connections. Communication serves as the bridge that turns intention into action, aiming to ensure that every member of your school community feels informed, included, and empowered.

Building Bridges Through Effective Communication

Effective communication is the key to fostering and sustaining successful special education programs. It provides staff with clear avenues for sharing feedback and receiving timely, accessible information. In special education, where clarity and empathy are vital, mastering the art of communication can profoundly enhance your school's culture. The goal is simple: Create an environment where every voice is heard, understood, and respected. Effective communication fosters a sense of belonging, transforming a good school culture into a great one.

The following list details practical strategies to enhance communication.

- **Open dialogue:** Build trust through consistent staff meetings and open-door policies. Open dialogue is the foundation of trust and collaboration in your school community. It involves speaking, active listening, and demonstrating understanding. When leaders model open dialogue, they set the tone for transparency and inclusivity.

- **Empathy and understanding:** Practice empathetic listening and schedule regular check-ins to show genuine care for staff well-being. Empathy in communication goes far beyond just hearing words; it's about understanding the emotions behind them. Special educators often face unique challenges, and showing empathy can help build strong, supportive relationships.

- **Information sharing:** Communicate updates through newsletters, establish clear protocols, and use visual aids to ensure clarity. Clear and consistent information sharing is crucial in a school environment. It prevents misunderstandings and aims to ensure that everyone is on the same page.

- **Feedback channels:** Provide surveys, suggestion boxes, forums, and anonymous platforms to encourage inclusive feedback. Creating multiple channels for feedback ensures that everyone has a voice. This can lead to more comprehensive and inclusive improvements.

I've seen firsthand how powerful effective communication can be in transforming schools into places where every member feels valued, heard, and informed. Through open dialogue, empathy, clear information sharing, and robust feedback channels, we can build bridges that support and sustain our educators and students alike.

Tips From the Top

As a leader, your actions set the tone for fostering a sense of belonging and partnership within your school community. This section offers practical, high-level strategies to address the challenges discussed in this chapter. I intend for these actionable insights to help you foster meaningful connections, empower your staff, and create a culture where mentorship and collaboration thrive.

- **Cultivate a culture of connection:** Lead by example in building relationships. Spend time getting to know your staff, students, and families. Schedule regular check-ins with teachers to understand their needs and foster a sense of belonging.

- **Prioritize transparent communication:** Set the tone for open dialogue by sharing key updates regularly and encouraging feedback. Use multiple communication channels (staff meetings, emails, and informal conversations) to ensure clarity and accessibility.

- **Empower teacher leaders:** Identify and nurture teacher leaders by offering mentorship opportunities. Provide the training and resources they need to support their peers effectively while promoting a culture of collaboration.

- **Leverage mentorship as a tool for retention:** Pair new teachers—and teachers with need or desire—with experienced mentors using a structured matching process. Ensure mentorship programs include regular check-ins, professional development opportunities, and recognition for mentor contributions.

- **Model emotional intelligence:** Talk the talk and walk the walk! Demonstrate empathy, self-regulation, and active listening in all interactions. Encourage staff to adopt these skills in their classrooms to build stronger relationships with students and colleagues. Imagine the impact this will have on mentorships.

- **Embed connection into professional learning:** Make collaboration and communication integral to professional learning. Use group problem solving, role playing, and case studies to reinforce shared learning experiences.

- **Celebrate successes, big and small:** Recognize and celebrate achievements—whether it's a student's progress, a teacher's milestone, or a collaborative team's effort. Public acknowledgment builds morale and reinforces a positive culture.

Voices From the Field

The Voices From the Field sections feature stories from educators. I chose to include these stories not only to highlight best practices but also to honor the incredible individuals I've had the privilege to support and partner with over the years. Each story reflects the relationships that fuel meaningful change and reminds us that at the heart of education are the connections we build and nurture. As you read these accounts, I hope they inspire you as they have inspired me.

The following vignette is shared by Erika Stevens, a former general educator who transitioned to special education before becoming a program specialist in California. With a wealth of experience and a unique perspective, Erika supervised a team of thirty-five special education teachers and played a pivotal role in designing and implementing a mentorship program to support new hires. Her story highlights the critical importance of structured mentorship in supporting and retaining special education teachers—a central theme of this chapter. Erika's firsthand account demonstrates how thoughtful mentorship practices can address teacher attrition, foster leadership, and create a culture of collaboration and support.

MENTORSHIP IN ACTION

During my tenure as a high school program specialist overseeing a team of thirty-five special education teachers, our director recognized a crucial need: the establishment of a mentorship program for new hires. This initiative aimed to provide invaluable support to incoming teachers navigating the challenges of acclimating to a new school environment and mastering unfamiliar procedures and platforms, all while balancing a full-time teaching schedule and managing a caseload of twenty-eight students.

This decision stemmed from the feedback of past recruits, who expressed feeling overwhelmed by the demands of their roles and apprehensive about sharing their concerns with administration. Hence, the mentorship model was designed to pair each new teacher with a seasoned mentor, fostering a safe space for candid discussions and guidance without the fear of repercussions. Additionally, this program served the dual purpose of nurturing leadership skills among existing staff and facilitating succession planning.

To identify suitable mentors, a rigorous selection process was conducted, evaluating candidates based on their expertise as special education teachers, as well as their professionalism and interpersonal skills within the department. Four mentors were ultimately chosen to spearhead this initiative.

The impact of the mentorship program was remarkable, as evidenced by feedback gathered from new hires at the conclusion of the school year. Notably, the program significantly contributed to teacher retention, with eight out of nine new hires opting to continue their employment. Beyond formal metrics, the qualitative testimonials from both mentors and mentees underscored the depth of support and camaraderie fostered through this initiative. Mentees expressed gratitude for the consistent guidance and reassurance their mentors—who were readily available to address queries and help, regardless of their magnitude—provided for them.

In summary, the mentorship program emerged as a cornerstone of our institution, enriching the professional development journey of new hires while bolstering staff cohesion and retention rates.

—Erika Stevens, Program Specialist, California

 Takeaway Tool Kit

This chapter's tool kit offers a curated collection of actionable insights and practical strategies designed to support your leadership journey. This section includes multiple tools tailored to address key areas such as mentorship, professional growth, and school culture. Each tool is crafted to guide you step by step, ensuring that your efforts are intentional, effective, and aligned with the unique needs of your team.

Figure 1.4 (page 32) serves as a practical and user-friendly guide on how to support and mentor teachers, particularly in special education. This tool provides straightforward strategies to encourage professional growth and create a positive and inclusive school culture. As I described earlier, identifying the needs of your team is a critical first step in understanding staff challenges, reviewing current support systems, and gathering feedback from everyone involved so leaders can pinpoint what's working and what needs improvement. My hope is that the variety of guides and tools offered throughout this chapter will be helpful in your journey of leading special education.

Promoting work-life balance, recognizing achievements, and fostering a sense of belonging are also crucial elements. Regularly checking in, evaluating progress, and being open to change based on feedback ensure that support systems stay relevant and effective. By using these strategies, leaders can create a supportive environment that not only keeps teachers happy and engaged but also leads to better outcomes for students.

Examining Current Systems of Support		
Description	**Initial Action Step**	**Person(s) Responsible**
Conduct a Needs Assessment Begin by surveying staff to identify their current needs and challenges. Use anonymous surveys, focus groups, and one-on-one interviews to gather comprehensive data. (This is discussed in depth in chapter 2, page 37.)		
Analyze Existing Support Structures Review current mentorship programs, professional development opportunities, and communication channels. Identify strengths and areas for improvement.		
Collect Feedback From Stakeholders Gather feedback from teachers, staff, parents, and students on existing support systems. Their insights can highlight gaps and potential enhancements.		

Developing and Enhancing Mentorship Programs		
Description	**Initial Action Step**	**Person(s) Responsible**
Set Clear Objectives Define the goals of your mentorship program. These might include improving teacher retention, fostering professional growth, and enhancing student outcomes.		
Pair Mentors and Mentees Thoughtfully Match mentors and mentees based on experience, teaching style, and personal interests to ensure compatibility and effective support.		

Description	Initial Action Step	Person(s) Responsible
Provide Training for Mentors Equip mentors with the skills they need to support their mentees effectively. Offer training sessions on active listening, constructive feedback, and professional guidance.		
Establish Regular Check-Ins Schedule consistent meetings between mentors and mentees to monitor progress, address challenges, and celebrate successes.		
Create a Supportive Community Foster a sense of community among mentors and mentees by organizing group activities, workshops, and social events.		

Implementing Techniques That Foster Healthy and Respectful Connections

Description	Initial Action Step	Person(s) Responsible
Exercise Active Listening Practice truly understanding the speaker's message, showing your team their insights are invaluable and critical to the school's success.		
Demonstrate Transparency Regularly share updates about school operations, challenges, and plans. This honesty establishes trust and fosters a shared responsibility for achieving the school's goals.		
Communicate Consistently Maintain regular communication with all staff members. Consistent dialogue inspires innovation and addresses potential issues early on.		

continued >

Figure 1.4: Actionable insights worksheet for leadership success.

Description	Initial Action Step	Person(s) Responsible
Establish a Judgment-Free Environment Encourage an atmosphere where sharing ideas and concerns is natural. Ensure everyone feels safe to speak up without fear of judgment.		
Celebrate Diversity Value the diverse backgrounds within your school as a source of strength and enrichment. Promote an environment where every difference is seen as an opportunity for learning and growth.		

Creating a Culture of Support and Belonging

Description	Initial Action Step	Person(s) Responsible
Promote Collective Decision Making Involve staff in decision-making processes to foster a sense of ownership and commitment to the school's mission.		
Recognize and Celebrate Achievements Regularly acknowledge and celebrate the accomplishments of staff and students to build morale and a sense of community.		
Offer Professional Learning Opportunities Provide ongoing training and development opportunities tailored to the needs and interests of your staff. (This is discussed more in depth in chapter 2, page 37).		
Support Work-Life Balance Encourage a healthy work-life balance by promoting wellness initiatives and flexible scheduling options.		

Visit go.SolutionTree.com/specialneeds for a free reproducible version of this figure.

Wrap-Up

Reflect on the moments in your career when you felt most connected and supported. These moments likely involved relationships that transcended the daily tasks and challenges of teaching. They are a testament to the enduring power of human connection in education. As you move forward, aspire to create an environment where such moments are the norm rather than the exception. Prioritize the development of mentorship programs, commit to transparent and empathetic communication, and foster a culture of inclusivity and support. By doing so, you will foster a resilient and thriving school community that benefits everyone involved.

Chapter Two

Investing in Professional Learning

Envision a school culture where every teacher and school administrator harnesses the full potential of professional development to thrive in their roles and profoundly impact the lives of diverse learners. This would be a school where professional learning is enjoyable and integrated into common school practice—a place where teachers feel empowered by targeted workshops, collaborative planning sessions, and real-time coaching. Imagine educators engaging in meaningful discussions about their experiences, sharing insights across teams, and immediately applying new knowledge to support diverse learners. This chapter emphasizes the critical role of school leaders in spearheading this movement, advocating for ongoing professional learning to cultivate an environment where the best educational practices are not just envisioned but enacted.

Existing research points to professional development and systems of support as being factors most salient to the retention of special educators (Billingsley et al., 2019; Levin, Berg-Jacobson, Atchison, Lee, & Vontsolos, 2015; Robinson et al., 2019). Research by Jessica L. Hagaman and Kathryn J. Casey (2018) highlights that while administrative support, recognition, and professional development are commonly cited reasons for attrition, school administrators often underestimate the impact of heavy caseloads and the need for specialized training. This gap in perception suggests the need for a more nuanced approach to supporting special educators, particularly in recognizing and addressing the specific challenges they face in their roles.

Bonnie Billingsley and Elizabeth Bettini are leading experts in special education and most known for their influential research on teacher retention, working conditions, and instructional practices that support educators and students with disabilities. They highlight the pivotal role of ongoing professional development in fostering teacher retention (Billingsley & Bettini, 2019). Their findings suggest that well-prepared teachers are less likely to leave the profession, largely due to enhanced job satisfaction and reduced stress.

This calls for a shift in how we support our educators; it's not just about offering support but tailoring it to meet the unique challenges of special education. By bridging the gap in perception between school leaders and special educators, recognizing the need for specialized training, and acknowledging the realities special educators face, we can cultivate a more supportive and understanding school environment that encourages longevity and satisfaction in educators' careers. Specialized training is not a need unique to special educators. Much research highlights all educators need tailored development that targets meeting the needs of diverse learners, namely students with disabilities (Byrd & Alexander, 2020; Crouse, Rice, & Mellard, 2016, 2018; Grimsby, 2020; Olechowska, 2020; Sheppard & Wieman, 2020; Zagona, Kurth, & MacFarland, 2017).

As school leaders, our role is not only to recognize the need for specialized training but to actively foster an environment where professional learning thrives, bridging the gap between current practice and the ideal standards of support and preparation that these dedicated educators truly need. By enhancing the ongoing development of educators through targeted training, we can address the critical shortage and high turnover rates. The following sections guide you to ensure professional learning and job-embedded training are parts of your plan to support special education teachers.

The Ongoing Professional Learning Framework

The success of our schools hinges on our collective ability to deliver effective and engaging professional learning experiences. It's about building a community where continuous growth and collaborative learning aren't just encouraged—they're embedded in the fabric of our school culture. To support you in this mission, the ongoing professional learning framework detailed in this section specifically guides the design of in-service models that are tailored to meet these needs so that professional development is ongoing and deeply integrated into the daily life of our schools. Following this, the framework further extends to job-embedded professional development, which emphasizes the practical application of these strategies directly within the teaching environment, fostering real-time learning and immediate application in the physical or virtual classroom space.

The ongoing professional learning framework is a comprehensive approach to nurturing continuous professional learning in your school community. Grounded in the influential research of Linda Darling-Hammond, Maria E. Hyler, and Madelyn Gardner (2017), it highlights the critical elements that make professional development truly impactful. Darling-Hammond's work, renowned for its deep dive into effective strategies, serves as a backbone for our framework. I've tailored this approach to help you lead and inspire, aiming to ensure that every professional learning experience is meaningful and directly applicable to the challenges and opportunities you face in your schools.

The ongoing professional learning framework, as shown in figure 2.1, emphasizes a holistic approach to professional learning, weaving together needs assessment, interactive workshops, expert-led coaching and support sessions, reflective practice, and ongoing evaluation. This framework illustrates a continuous, cyclical process for addressing professional development. Each component is designed to support and enhance the educational journey of your team, with the hope that it supports you leading your team through effective evolution and positive outcomes in your school community.

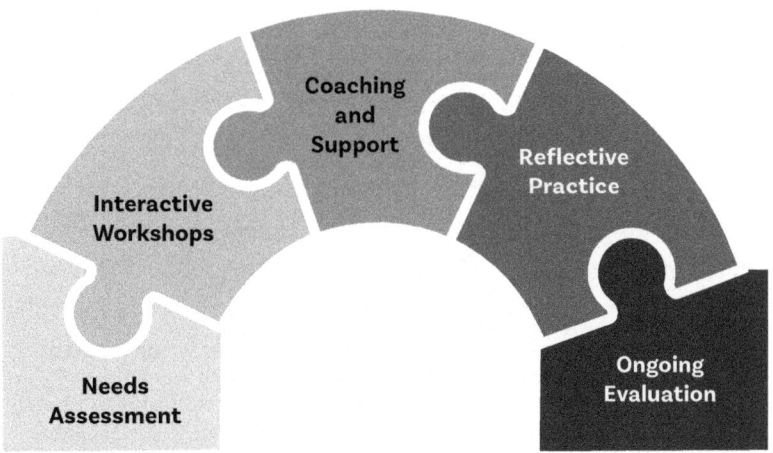

Source: © 2024 by CollaborativeEd Solutions.
Figure 2.1: The ongoing professional learning framework.

This framework is designed to support leaders in planning and executing the continuous development of educators through stages of a needs assessment, interactive workshops, coaching and support, reflective practice, and ongoing evaluation, aiming to ensure professional learning is both dynamic and responsive to the needs of educators. This framework is applicable to online, hybrid, and brick-and-mortar school environments. In the following sections, I break down each critical element of the framework and provide ways you can meet these objectives.

Needs Assessment

Needs assessment is, first and foremost, a process—one that can help education leaders successfully address education challenges. A *needs assessment* involves collecting and utilizing information to make informed decisions about the value and direction of a program or method (Stufflebeam, McCormick, Brinkerhoff, & Nelson, 1985). Prioritizing this first step helps us tailor professional learning experiences to meet the specific needs and desires of our educators and students. To emphasize how crucial this initial step is in setting the direction for relevant and impactful learning experiences, I've included a needs assessment guide at the end of this chapter in the Takeaway Tool Kit section (page 60).

Conducting a thorough needs assessment enables education leaders to make informed decisions that will drive relevant, impactful, and targeted learning experiences for all. The following are actions you can take to help meet this objective.

- **Develop a comprehensive needs assessment plan:** Outline the objectives, tools, and timelines for the needs assessment. Define clear goals that specify what information you need to inform the professional development programs.

- **Use diverse data collection methods:** Employ a variety of methods to gather and review data, including surveys, interviews, focus groups, and observations. Ensure these tools are designed to capture a broad spectrum of needs across different educator roles and learning environments while maintaining a focus on your targeted areas.

- **Engage stakeholders in the process:** Actively involve a range of stakeholders in the needs assessment process, including teachers, administrators, support staff, community members, and possibly students. Their input is crucial to understanding the multifaceted needs within the school.

- **Analyze existing data:** Review existing data sources such as student performance metrics, engagement metrics, previous professional development feedback, and other artifacts. This review can highlight ongoing challenges and areas needing attention.

- **Identify priority areas:** Analyze the collected data to identify critical areas where professional development and resources are most needed. Prioritization helps focus resources on areas that will have the most significant impact on educational outcomes.

- **Report findings to stakeholders:** Summarize the findings in a clear and actionable report that communicates the identified needs to applicable stakeholders. Transparency in this process fosters stakeholder commitment and support for subsequent improvement initiatives.

- **Set actionable goals for professional development:** Based on the needs assessment findings, set specific, measurable, attainable, results-oriented, and time-bound (SMART) goals for your professional development programs (Conzemius & O'Neill, 2014) and determine who you will partner with to achieve these goals. These goals should directly address the identified needs.

- **Review and revise regularly:** Establish a regular review cycle for the needs assessment process to ensure that it remains up-to-date with the evolving needs of the school community. Continuous improvement will enhance the relevance and effectiveness of professional development initiatives.

Figure 2.2 (page 42) is a critical tool designed to guide school leaders and educators in systematically identifying and addressing the specific needs in their school context. This reflection tool aims to ensure that professional learning initiatives are precisely tailored to meet the unique challenges and opportunities present in your school community. By considering the essential questions provided, you can lay a strong foundation for an effective needs assessment process that drives strategic planning, policy development, allocation of resources, and program implementation.

> **Essential Questions**
>
> What are the primary goals you hope to achieve through this needs assessment?
>
> Which stakeholders will you include?
>
> What is the preferred timeline? Are there any critical dates that you must consider (for example, parent-teacher conferences, state assessments, school closures, and so on)?
>
> Are there any limitations or constraints that you need to consider in the planning, execution, and reporting processes?
>
> Have you conducted similar assessments in the past? If so, what were the key findings, and how did you address them? Can you access previous assessment data to inform the current assessment?
>
> What existing data do you already have that can inform the needs assessment? How will you facilitate access to additional necessary data (such as student performance data and program evaluation reports)?
>
> How do you envision you will share findings and recommendations with stakeholders?
>
> How do you intend to use the findings from the needs assessment? Is there a process in place for integrating findings into strategic planning, policy development, and program implementation?
>
> Are there known challenges or barriers that could impact the success of the needs assessment? How might you mitigate these?
>
> Who will be involved in conducting the needs assessment?

Source: State Support Network, 2018.
Figure 2.2: Needs assessment starter reflection guide.
Visit go.SolutionTree.com/specialneeds for a free reproducible version of this figure.

Engaging in this reflective process will help you clarify your goals, involve critical stakeholders, and develop a realistic timeline. Needs assessments should be uniquely designed to study the needs of your context in relation to your goals. Ultimately, my hope is that the insights you gain from this reflection will support informed decision making and foster a collaborative approach to continuous improvement in teaching and learning.

Interactive Workshops

Next, use the insights from your needs assessment to craft targeted interactive workshops that address your identified training needs effectively. These workshops are designed to provide active, hands-on learning experiences that engage educators through discussion, simulations, and problem-solving activities tailored to areas requiring enhancement. Programs that actively involve teachers in learning and applying new skills are generally more successful. Involve your teachers and other staff, where possible, as leaders of workshops. Together, workshops led by teachers and external consultants form a cohesive learning experience that not only addresses immediate educational challenges but also equips educators with new methods and techniques to elevate their teaching effectiveness. As the founder of CollaborativeEd Solutions, I've had the honor and delight of partnering with teachers to facilitate professional learning workshops for teachers within the school community.

Your workshops should aim to engage educators actively and dynamically using methods that encourage participation and practical application of new skills. The following are actions you can take to meet this objective.

- **Customize workshop content:** Tailor the workshop content to directly address the specific needs you identified in the needs assessment. This involves customizing scenarios, activities, and discussion topics to reflect the actual challenges and opportunities within your educational environment.

- **Engage expert facilitators:** Involve expert facilitators who not only have deep knowledge in their subject areas but also possess strong facilitation skills. These experts should be capable of engaging educators dynamically, and they can adapt their delivery based on the responses of the workshop participants. Leverage your own staff when possible!

- **Use diverse teaching methods:** Incorporate a variety of teaching methods in the workshops to cater to different learning styles. Include demonstrations, group discussions, and interactive simulations to make learning experiential and memorable.

- **Provide practical tools and resources:** Equip educators with practical tools, templates, and resources they can use immediately in their teaching practice. These could include lesson plans, assessment tools, or digital resources that support the implementation of new strategies they learned during the workshops.

- **Foster collaborative learning environments:** Create a supportive and collaborative learning environment where educators feel safe to express ideas, ask questions, and share experiences. Facilitate peer learning by organizing small group activities that encourage collaboration and peer feedback.

Figure 2.3 is a resource for school leaders to design and execute engaging workshops that facilitate active learning among educators. This guide

Session Overview

Workshop Title: _____
Date and Time: _____ Facilitator: _____
Target Audience: _____

Workshop Objectives:
1._____
2._____
3._____

Session Agenda

Time	Activity	Description
	Welcome and Introduction	Opening remarks and workshop overview
	Meaningful Icebreaker or Restorative Activity	Engaging activity to start the session
	Main Activity 1	(Title of the activity)
	Main Activity 2	(Title of the activity)
	Break	
	Main Activity 3	(Title of the activity)
	Q&A	Time allocated for questions and answers
	Wrap-Up and Reflection	Summary of key takeaways and time for participant reflection

Activity Planning Template

Activity Title: _____
Objective: _____
Description: _____
Materials Needed: _____
Timing: _____
Instructions:
1._____
2._____
3._____

Examples of Effective Workshop Activities

Role Plays
Objective: _____
Example Scenario: _____

Instructions:
1. Assign roles to participants.
2. Provide a scenario.
3. Facilitate a role-play session.
4. Debrief to discuss outcomes and learning points.

Simulations
Objective: _____
Example Scenario: _____

Instructions:
1. Set up the simulation environment.
2. Guide participants through the simulation.
3. Debrief to discuss outcomes and learning points.

Group Discussions
Objective: _____
Example Topic: _____

Instructions:
1 Divide participants into small groups.
2. Provide discussion prompts.
3. Facilitate a group discussion.
4. Summarize the key points each group shared.

Tips for Integrating Digital Tools

Interactive Polls
Tool: Mentimeter, Poll Everywhere, Nearpod (for example)
Tip: Use polls to gather participant opinions or quiz them on workshop content.

Virtual Breakout Rooms
Tool: Zoom, Microsoft Teams (for example)
Tip: Use breakout rooms for small group discussions or activities during virtual workshops.

Multimedia Presentations
Tool: Prezi, PowerPoint, Genially, generative AI (for example)
Tip: Incorporate videos, animations, and interactive elements to make presentations more engaging.

After each workshop, remember to gather feedback from your participants. Their insights are invaluable in helping you improve future sessions. Use this feedback to refine and enhance your workshops, ensuring they continue to meet the needs of your educators and drive meaningful professional development. Your commitment to continuous improvement will make a significant difference in the success of your programs.

Figure 2.3: Interactive workshop planning guide.

*Visit **go.SolutionTree.com/specialneeds** for a free reproducible version of this figure.*

provides step-by-step instructions, templates, and tips for planning workshops that are interactive and impactful. It covers everything from topic selection to activity design and the integration of technology to enhance engagement. This planning guide is not intended to train you on effective workshop execution. I am extremely passionate about effective facilitation of any professional learning experience; to dive deeply into this topic is beyond the scope of this chapter, but this guide provides you with an excellent place to start.

Coaching and Support

After the energizing activities of the interactive workshops, coaching and support step in as crucial elements for sustaining the momentum of learning. This phase is designed to support educators as they begin to apply their new knowledge and skills in their teaching environments. Effective coaching provides personalized guidance to help educators overcome the specific challenges they face when implementing new strategies or enhance their current pedagogy. This support is not a one-time intervention; rather, it's an ongoing process that adapts to the evolving needs of the educators, ensuring the professional growth sparked in workshops continues to evolve into lasting change.

It's important to offer sustained support and individualized coaching to educators following interactive workshops to ensure the practical application of learned strategies and the continuous development of teaching skills. The following are actions you can take to meet this objective.

- **Provide targeted coaching support:** Pair educators with coaches who can provide targeted feedback and one-on-one support as they implement new teaching practices.

- **Address implementation challenges:** Organize follow-up sessions that address specific implementation challenges or provide targeted enhancement to offer solutions and alternative approaches that foster effective teaching.

- **Leverage digital communication tools:** Use digital platforms to maintain communication and support between coaches and educators, facilitating timely advice and encouragement. Time constraints are a common barrier to success!

Figure 2.4 is a resource designed to assist you or your designated coaching team in providing targeted, evidence-based coaching to special education teachers. By following this structured approach and tailoring it to meet the unique needs of your context, you can more effectively support them in enhancing their instructional practices, managing IEPs effectively, and building their professional skills for sustained success. Your teachers deserve this support.

The following guide includes instructions and practical tools for onboarding discussions, goal setting, instructional enhancement, technology integration, advocacy, and more. It aims to empower teachers with the knowledge and skills they need to meet the diverse needs of their students and to continue their professional growth independently. As always, use what is applicable to your context and amend the tool to meet your unique needs. Remember, leverage your needs assessment data to guide your coaching initiatives and don't forget about mentors as a form of coaching. Keep your mentors in mind as you plan ongoing development for mentees.

Onboarding Discussion and Initial Observation
- **Purpose:** Establish a baseline understanding of the teacher's current practices and specific challenges.
- **Actions:**
  - Identify and address specific challenges and needs unique to special education.
  - Apply evidence-based strategies to enhance instructional practices for students with diverse learning needs.
  - Improve universal instruction techniques to improve accessibility for all learners.

Goal Setting and Planning
- **Purpose:** Collaboratively set personalized goals and develop action plans.
- **Actions:**
  - Set personalized goals aligned with professional development needs.
  - Develop action plans to implement targeted strategies that align with special education best practices.
  - Establish measurable outcomes for continuous improvement in instructional effectiveness.

Instructional Effectiveness and IEP Management Skills
- **Purpose:** Provide targeted coaching based on the teacher's specific needs.
- **Actions:**
  - Instructional Effectiveness:
    - Address specific challenges and needs unique to special education.
    - Apply evidence-based strategies to enhance instructional practices.
    - Improve universal instruction techniques.
    - Address co-planning with shared educators and providers of services.
  - IEP Management:

continued >

Figure 2.4: Active coaching and support guide.

- Develop proficiency in creating and maintaining IEPs.
- Strengthen collaboration with multidisciplinary teams.
- Apply strategic planning to monitor, assess, and adjust IEPs.

Individualized Feedback and Reflection
- **Purpose:** Provide constructive feedback and engage in reflective practices.
- **Actions:**
  - Receive individualized feedback on instructional techniques and classroom management.
  - Engage in reflective practices to enhance self-awareness and professional growth.
  - Explore strategies to address challenges and capitalize on strengths.

Technology Use
- **Purpose:** Integrate technology to enhance special education practices.
- **Actions:**
  - Explore virtual or in-person tools and resources for differentiated instruction and IEP meetings.
  - Integrate technology to support individualized learning plans.
  - Develop proficiency in leveraging technology for remote or in-person instruction.

Advocacy and Collaboration Skills
- **Purpose:** Strengthen advocacy and collaboration within the school community.
- **Actions:**
  - Strengthen advocacy skills for students with special needs.
  - Foster effective collaboration with colleagues, administrators, and parents.
  - Develop strategies to communicate the unique contributions of special education.

Coaching Journey Wrap-Up and Independence Building
- **Purpose:** Facilitate a comprehensive review and plan for sustained professional practices.
- **Actions:**
  - Review the coaching journey, highlighting accomplishments and areas for growth.
  - Develop a plan for sustained professional practices beyond coaching sessions.
  - Equip teachers with self-assessment tools and resources for continued professional development.
  - Foster a sense of ownership and confidence in implementing effective practices independently.
  - Provide ongoing support mechanisms to ensure sustained success after the coaching engagement concludes.

*Visit **go.SolutionTree.com/specialneeds** for a free reproducible version of this figure.*

Reflective Practice

Reflective practice allows educators to pause and reflect on their pedagogy, which facilitates a culture of continuous improvement and contributes to professional growth. Finnish education models are known for prioritizing professional development. A study in Finland discovered that reflective practices enhance novice teachers' self-awareness and teaching practices (Mathew, Mathew, & Peechattu, 2017). Consider integrating reflective practices into your professional learning initiatives. Some possibilities include structured reflective time during workshops, follow-up reflection meetings, peer sharing circles, self-observations, and reflective journals (Kennedy, 2016). The following are actions you can take to meet this objective.

- **Schedule structured reflective sessions:** Organize regular, dedicated times before, during, and after professional learning experiences for educators to reflect on their experiences and insights.
- **Facilitate peer sharing circles:** Establish groups where educators can share their teaching experiences and reflections in a supportive environment, fostering collaborative learning.
- **Encourage self-observation:** Guide educators to record and review their own teaching sessions to self-assess and identify areas for improvement.
- **Implement reflective journals:** Provide educators with journals to document their reflections, offering prompts that help guide their thoughts toward effective pedagogical practices.
- **Conduct follow-up reflection meetings:** Arrange and encourage meetings where educators can discuss the outcomes of their reflections and the application of new strategies in their classrooms.
- **Provide training on reflective techniques:** Offer specific training sessions that focus on enhancing educators' reflective practices, including how to effectively use feedback from peers and self-assessments.

Figure 2.5 (page 50) is a structured tool designed to facilitate regular reflection among educators. These journal prompts will aid in recording insights from professional development activities, tracking progress in implementing new strategies, and reflecting on teaching practices and outcomes. By systematically engaging in reflective practice, educators can enhance their professional growth and effectiveness.

Learning Reflection:
1. What are the key takeaways from today's professional learning activity?

2. How does the new information align with or challenge your current teaching practices?

3. In what ways can you apply what you have learned to your classroom?

Challenges Reflection:
4. What challenges did you encounter when trying to implement new strategies?

5. How did you address these challenges?

6. What support do you need to overcome these obstacles?

Success Reflection:
7. What successes have you experienced since the last reflection?

8. What factors contributed to these successes?

9. How can you build on these positive outcomes?

Action Plan:

10. Describe the new strategy or technique you plan to implement.

11. Describe how you will implement this strategy.

    - By what date: _____
    - Resources needed:

12. Define what you hope to achieve.

13. Outline how you will measure success.

Future Professional Learning Needs:

14. Specify a specific professional development goal you want to achieve.

15. List the steps you plan to take to work toward achieving this goal.
    Step 1:

    Step 2:

    Step 3:

    Step 4:

16. Describe the resources you will need.

17. Set a timeline for achieving your goal.

Figure 2.5: Reflection and post-learning action guide.

*Visit **go.SolutionTree.com/specialneeds** for a free reproducible version of this figure.*

Ongoing Evaluation

Finally, ongoing evaluation is pivotal in assessing the effectiveness of our professional development initiatives. When we continuously measure the impact of professional development on teaching practices, school culture, and student outcomes, we create an integral feedback loop that not only informs necessary adjustments but also validates the progress and success of our efforts. Crafting a systematic approach aims to ensure that our professional development remains aligned with our educational goals and responsive to both educator and student needs, thereby reinforcing the foundation for sustained improvement and excellence in teaching.

It's helpful to systematically assess the effectiveness of professional development activities to ensure they positively impact teaching practices and student outcomes. This continuous evaluation is essential to validate progress, guide necessary adjustments, and sustain overall improvement in educational quality. The following are actions you can take to meet this objective.

- **Implement regular assessment cycles:** Establish a schedule for regular assessments of your professional development's impact, using both quantitative and qualitative data to measure changes in teaching practices and student learning outcomes.

- **Use diverse evaluation tools:** Employ a variety of tools such as surveys, teacher assessments, student performance data, and observational checklists to gather comprehensive feedback on the effectiveness of training programs.

- **Have feedback integration meetings:** Organize meetings where educators and administrators can discuss evaluation results and provide feedback on the professional development they received. This helps refine future PD initiatives and address specific needs.

- **Adapt and refine professional development programs:** Based on evaluation outcomes, adjust and tailor professional development programs to better meet the evolving needs of educators and students. Ensure these changes are data-driven and aligned with overarching educational goals.

- **Report and communicate results:** Regularly communicate the findings from ongoing evaluations to all stakeholders, including teachers, school leaders, and possibly parents and community members to maintain transparency and collective buy-in.

- **Document successes and challenges:** Keep a detailed record of successes and areas for improvement identified through evaluations to inform long-term planning and support continuous quality improvement in professional development efforts.

As we consider these action steps, it's important to reflect on the foundational principles we've already discussed: clear goals, targeted strategies, and strong stakeholder engagement. By integrating these elements into your evaluation process, you can ensure that your professional development initiatives not only meet their immediate objectives but also contribute to lasting educational excellence.

Following are some critical questions to consider. These are designed to help you assess the current state of your professional development programs and think strategically about implementing the ongoing professional learning framework. Engaging with these questions will help you pinpoint areas of strength as well as opportunities for growth, ensuring that your professional development efforts are as impactful as possible. Let's take a moment to reflect on these aspects before moving forward to the next section of our journey.

- How effectively are you identifying the professional development needs of your teachers?
- Reflect on the most recent professional development workshop conducted at your school. What elements worked well, and what could be improved?
- How do you currently evaluate the impact of professional development activities on teaching practices and student outcomes?
- In what ways are you facilitating reflective practice among your teachers?
- How does this framework align with your school's or district's current professional development policies and practices?

Having established the importance of ongoing evaluation as a cornerstone for effective professional development programming, it's equally vital to consider how professional learning can become an integral part of educators' daily routines. Evaluation informs us of what works, and embedding that knowledge into day-to-day practices leads to sustainable and impactful professional development. This is where job-embedded training emerges as a transformative approach. When we integrate learning opportunities into the fabric of teaching, this job-embedded training moves professional development from isolated events to a continuous process that fosters growth, collaboration, and innovation. Let's talk about components I believe are key to this approach and explore how it can elevate both individual and collective teaching practices.

Job-Embedded Training

At the heart of effective educational leadership is the capacity to embed continuous professional learning within the day-to-day activities of teaching. Job-embedded training is a strategic and integrative approach designed to fuse professional learning seamlessly into the fabric of daily instructional practices. This avenue of professional learning goes beyond our traditional coaching and workshop–style ways of learning. Job-embedded training can serve as an extension of other sources of training and development and is intended to support your team's professional goals.

This approach leverages innovative technology as a critical enabler to ensure that professional development is both accessible and deeply integrated within all teaching environments. It transforms the concept of learning from an isolated event to an ongoing, synchronized process that enhances both teaching and learning across the board. Research supports its effectiveness in enhancing both teaching quality and student outcomes. A 2023 meta-analysis found that job-embedded professional development has a significant, medium-to-large effect on teacher performance and a medium effect on student achievement, a finding that supports the implementation of job-embedded professional development programs in schools (Balta, Fukkink, & Amendum, 2023). Additionally, the National Institute for Excellence in Teaching (2012) emphasizes that while job-embedded professional development can improve instruction and student learning, its success depends on a robust infrastructure to support, oversee, and reinforce these initiatives.

The following are key components to implementing job-embedded training.

- **Co-teaching and co-planning:** Embedded directly into daily teaching environments, this strategy unites general and special education teachers in the classroom to collaboratively plan and execute lessons. This integration goes beyond mere physical co-location, as this approach can effectively be implemented in hybrid and online learning environments. It strategically combines diverse expertise to significantly enhance educational outcomes for all students. As a dynamic form of on-the-job training, co-teaching and co-planning facilitate the immediate application of inclusive teaching strategies, provide real-time problem-solving opportunities, and foster a culture of mutual professional growth. By working closely together, teachers continuously learn from each other, instantly applying collaborative insights and shared practices that reflect a commitment to inclusive education (Friend & Cook, 2017). We will go into more detail on co-teaching and co-planning in chapter 3 (page 63).

- **Structured observations:** Central to this framework lies a system of structured observations encompassing both peer observations and self-observations. Teachers observe each other's classes (Darling-Hammond et al., 2017) and record their own lessons to review later. This dual approach allows educators to engage in in-depth reflective feedback sessions and focus on promoting inclusivity and effective differentiation in teaching. By watching their own recorded sessions, teachers can self-assess and identify specific areas for enhancement, while peer reviews provide external perspectives that encourage openness and foster a culture of continuous professional development. Together, these practices help educators refine their teaching methods through constructive collegial input, underpinning a commitment to lifelong improvement (Zagona et al., 2017).

- **Asynchronous training tools:** Recognizing the diverse schedules and learning paces of educators, this element highlights a digital opportunity to create a virtual library stocked with training modules, video tutorials, and additional resources. Available on demand, teachers can enhance their skills at their own pace and according to their own needs. As a school leader, you can also use this space to assign teachers training materials aligned to support their professional growth. For example, your library might cover topics ranging from classroom management to advanced inclusive teaching techniques and house quick-reference guides, recordings, articles, websites, and so on. Consider leveraging the strengths of your teaching team by storing brief recordings in your library of your teachers executing effective practices. This can also be done individually—meaning, you may need to provide an individual teacher with personalized virtual learning experiences and resources. Finally, it is essential to identify team members to manage the virtual library to ensure equitable access and materials for all.

- **Virtual coaching:** Videoconferencing technology can be used to facilitate personalized virtual coaching sessions and strategically connect teachers with experts, both inside and outside your organization, who provide customized guidance and support. Virtual coaching can be leveraged to overcome geographical and logistical hurdles, ensuring that teachers receive timely and focused support and empowerment (Zimmer & Matthews, 2022). This approach not only aids in the swift implementation of new strategies but also enriches teachers' technological competencies. In my experience, platforms such as Loom (www.loom.com), Genially (https://genially.com), and GoReact (https://get.goreact.com) are effective in delivering this coaching. Wendi K. Zimmer and Sharon D. Matthews (2022) highlight a significant advantage of virtual coaching: Teachers receiving this form of support are more likely to actively explore and incorporate new technological tools into their teaching practices, enhancing their digital fluency and instructional methods.

Job-embedded training is designed to make professional development a natural, integrated part of educators' daily lives, where technology enhances access and collaboration. Reflecting on the implementation and impact of job-embedded training is crucial for its success and for the continuous growth of your educational community. The following reflection questions are designed to help you critically assess the integration of this approach in your school, identify areas of strength, and pinpoint opportunities for further enhancement. Engaging with these questions will provide valuable insights that can guide the ongoing development of your professional learning initiatives, ensuring they remain aligned with both educator needs and institutional goals. Let's reflect on these aspects to ensure that our commitment to professional growth translates to tangible benefits for our educators and students alike. If these are reflection questions you need time to ponder, please take the time you need. If you find that one or more are not relevant to your team, I encourage you to replace them with more applicable questions that will guide your team's professional growth.

- How effectively have you integrated co-teaching and co-planning in your school? What successes or challenges have you observed, and how can you improve these strategies?
- In what ways are you utilizing structured observations—peer and self-observations—to promote reflective practice and professional growth? Are they meeting your goals?
- Assess the utilization and accessibility of your virtual library and other asynchronous training tools. Are teachers effectively leveraging these resources to enhance their skills?
- Evaluate the impact of coaching on your teachers' professional growth. How well is this approach providing tailored support and empowering educators to innovate?
- Reflect on the overall integration of the job-embedded training framework within your professional development programs. What impact has it had on teaching and learning, and what steps can you take to ensure its continued evolution?

Reflecting on the integration and effectiveness of job-embedded training provides valuable insights into the current state of your professional development initiatives and guides necessary adjustments. As you continue to refine and implement these practices, it's equally important to address the common challenges that often arise in professional development, such as limited resources, time constraints, and resistance to change.

To help you navigate these hurdles, the following section offers actionable strategies designed to foster healthy engagement, motivation, and sustained professional growth. These insights are crafted to ensure that your professional development efforts remain relevant, accessible, and impactful for your educators and students.

 Tips From the Top

In addition to the ideas shared throughout this chapter, I'd like to provide guidance to support your approach. This section offers actionable strategies to address common hurdles such as limited resources, time constraints, and resistance to change. These high-level insights cover learning experiences that are relevant, accessible, and impactful.

- **Maximize limited resources.**
  - Take advantage of free or low-cost platforms like webinars, massive open online courses (MOOCs), and educational websites.
  - Foster collaborative peer-to-peer learning sessions to build a strong community of practice.
  - Seek grants or partner with universities and educational organizations to reduce training costs.
  - Embed professional development into daily activities. (Refer to the Job-Embedded Training section on page 54.)
- **Address time constraints.**
  - Incorporate professional development into planning periods or early-release days.
  - Leverage microlearning sessions (10–15 minutes) to fit busy schedules. These can be incredibly enriching!
  - Provide asynchronous learning options like recorded webinars and online courses for flexible access.
- **Overcome resistance to change.**
  - Involve teachers in planning to ensure relevance and address their needs.
  - Introduce new methods incrementally, allowing teachers to pilot strategies in small steps.
  - Create a supportive culture where innovation is encouraged and feedback is readily available.
- **Ensure relevance.**
  - Conduct regular needs assessments to identify areas where support is most needed.
  - Focus on hands-on workshops that offer practical tools and classroom-ready strategies.
  - Provide follow-up coaching to help teachers implement new techniques effectively.

- **Sustain motivation.**
  - Celebrate successes and acknowledge teachers' progress in professional development.
  - Allow teachers to personalize their professional development paths based on interests and career goals.
  - Offer diverse formats and topics to keep learning fresh, engaging, and relevant.

 Voices From the Field

The following vignette is shared by Lindsay, a credentialed special education teacher who has transitioned to a leadership role as a school administrator overseeing districtwide professional development and new-teacher training. With firsthand experience as both an online teacher and administrator, Lindsay offers a unique perspective on what effective professional learning looks like—learning that is interactive, targeted, and immediately applicable.

Her story reflects the central theme of this chapter: the importance of designing professional development that meets educators where they are, addresses their specific needs, and empowers them with tools they can implement right away. Lindsay's account demonstrates how thoughtful, well-structured workshops can not only transform teaching practices but also lead to meaningful improvements in student outcomes.

EFFECTIVE WORKSHOPS

Special educators know that learning happens in stages and isn't one-size-fits-all, yet professional learning often fails to reflect this. Traditional workshops typically involve presentations focusing only on knowledge acquisition. These sessions often result in paper handouts that end up gathering dust.

However, I was fortunate to experience an effective professional development program that offered targeted workshops and webinars throughout the school year. Educators were given a menu of PD options to choose from depending on their professional goal or the immediate needs within their classroom. I attended an in-person workshop that focused on using structured environments to help autistic students learn effectively.

Participants were asked to bring information about a specific student needing support. This made the workshop immediately relevant and interactive.

The presenter used a series of mini workshops: introducing topics, providing visual examples, discussing case studies, and then allowing educators time to apply what they learned to their specific student. We then collaborated with peers to refine our plans, receiving feedback and gaining new insights.

By the end of the day, I had not only acquired new strategies but also had practical resources ready to implement in my classroom, thereby addressing the (often overlooked) maintenance and generalization stages of learning. The next morning, I made immediate adjustments and shared the knowledge with my instructional team. While changes took time to become routine, my students eventually thrived, demonstrating the effectiveness of a workshop that addresses all stages of learning.

—Lindsay Scacco, School Administrator, California

 Takeaway Tool Kit

I cannot emphasize enough that implementing regular assessment cycles and using diverse evaluation tools are crucial steps in systematically evaluating the effectiveness of your programs. I've shared many guides and resources throughout this chapter, and the following two tools—the "Assessment Schedule" (figure 2.6) and "Assessment Checklist" (figure 2.7)—are the ones I'll leave you with as this chapter nears its end. By leveraging these tools, leaders can aim to ensure data collection is thorough, timely, and actionable, which I hope will guide necessary adjustments and improvements to ultimately enhance teaching practices and student outcomes.

 Wrap-Up

This chapter highlighted the critical importance of investing in professional learning for teachers. We began with the vision of a school culture where ongoing professional development is paramount, creating endless opportunities for educators to thrive and profoundly impact students with diverse learning needs. School leaders play a pivotal role in this movement, advocating for continuous learning to ensure the best educational practices are not just envisioned but enacted. If you couldn't already tell, I am not a fan of the "one-stop-shop" approach to professional learning that renowned researchers have warned us about for quite some time (Clarke & Hollingsworth, 2002; Darling-Hammond et al., 2017), and

Use this tool to plan and organize your regular assessment cycles. Make sure to address all key elements to ensure a systematic evaluation process. The first row shows an example.

Date	Focus Area	Data Collection Methods	Responsible Parties	Review Meeting Date	Actions Items
September 15, 2025	Teacher satisfaction	Surveys, focus groups	PD coordinator, teacher leaders	October 1, 2025	Address top three concerns; plan follow-up survey

Figure 2.6: Assessment schedule.

Visit **go.SolutionTree.com/specialneeds** for a free blank reproducible version of this figure.

Use this reflective checklist to ensure all necessary preparations and follow-ups are completed to maintain a thorough and organized assessment process. I encourage you to refine it to meet the unique needs of your context, especially considering the outcome of any needs assessment. This reflective guide will help get you started.

Preparation:
- Are all assessment tools prepared?
  ☐ Yes ☐ In progress ☐ No
- Have appropriate stakeholders been informed about the assessment schedule and purpose?
  ☐ Yes ☐ In progress ☐ No
- Is there a clear plan for data collection methods and timelines?
  ☐ Yes ☐ In progress ☐ No

Execution:
- Have you scheduled regular intervals for data collection?
  ☐ Yes ☐ In progress ☐ No
- Are there designated individuals responsible for collecting and compiling data?
  ☐ Yes ☐ In progress ☐ No

continued >

Figure 2.7: Assessment checklist.

> **Review:**
> - Is there a timeline for analyzing and reviewing data?
>   ☐ Yes   ☐ In progress   ☐ No
> - Have review meetings been scheduled and participants notified?
>   ☐ Yes   ☐ In progress   ☐ No
> - Are there specific criteria for evaluating the effectiveness of the PD initiatives?
>   ☐ Yes   ☐ In progress   ☐ No

*Visit **go.SolutionTree.com/specialneeds** for a free reproducible version of this figure.*

I urge professional leaders to consider the divine importance of long-duration and sustained professional learning.

Tailored and continuous professional learning should address the unique challenges special education teachers face, from heavy caseloads to the need for specialized guidance and support. By bridging the gap between school leaders' perceptions and the realities of special educators' roles, we can create a more supportive and effective teaching environment.

As we conclude this chapter, I hope it's clear that equipping educators with the tools and knowledge they need is essential for fostering growth and improving outcomes. In the next chapter, we'll explore how the collective pedagogy, by way of co-teaching and co-planning, can support further transformation of special education. These pedagogical models support teacher development and aim to foster inclusive environments where all students can thrive.

Chapter Three

Co-Teaching and Co-Planning

In the complex and ever-evolving world of education, educators work tirelessly to support students with diverse learning pathways. To empower our educators and enhance the overall success of special education programs, we must recognize the importance of what I call *collective pedagogy* through co-teaching and co-planning.

Collective pedagogy is a multifaceted concept that can embody various aspects. It is a teaching approach that emphasizes shared responsibility, collaborative decision making, and joint effort among educators to design, facilitate, and reflect on instructional practices. Collective pedagogy can manifest in countless ways, such as through interdisciplinary projects, team meetings, co-teaching and co-planning, mentorship programs, and professional learning communities. This emphasis on collective effort not only amplifies the impact of individual contributions but also lays the groundwork for building stronger, more effective connections across our school communities.

A study of eight high-performing school districts in California, one of which I've had the pleasure of partnering with, shines a light on the undeniable fact that when teachers from special and general education backgrounds work together, the students' academic results don't just get a little better—they drastically improve (Huberman, Navo, & Parrish, 2012). The state determined these school districts had above average special education performance, and their practices were linked to research and literature on effective pedagogy for neurodiverse student populations. Collective pedagogy between special and general educators was specifically cited as one of the effective strategies that led to above average student performance.

Following the insights from California's high-performing school districts, Eric E. Kobischen's (2020) study dives even deeper into what makes collective pedagogy so pivotal, especially in relation to the retention of special education teachers. This research homes in on key factors like interdependence, flexibility, and the creation of new professional activities that increase the likelihood of teachers experiencing success and maintaining their roles. Kobischen's (2020) findings highlight that intentional and structured collaboration between special and general educators significantly correlates with special education teachers' intent to stay in the profession. Collaborative practices create a supportive environment where special educators feel valued and connected, reducing feelings of isolation that often lead to burnout. The collective commitment among partner teachers contributes to the development of innovative teaching strategies, which are critical to fostering an inclusive learning environment.

In essence, when special and general education teachers unite around shared goals and reflect on their journey together, they're not just more likely to stay in their roles—they're also setting the stage for their success and that of their learners. This study isn't just a lone voice; it echoes a chorus of research underscoring the critical need for a collaborative culture in schools. Without it, we risk losing talented educators who are essential to our students' diverse learning needs.

Leaders like Anthony Muhammed, Linda Darling-Hammond, and Michael Fullan have championed the concept of collective pedagogy; their works on collaboration and collective commitment have been a driving force for systemic change in education. Their collective works underline the transformative power of collaborative effort and advocate for integrated strategies that support educators' professional growth and, as a natural extension, enhance student learning (Berry, Darling-Hammond, & Mackay, 2021; Fullan & Edwards, 2022; Muhammad, 2009, 2024). Let's also consider the insights of someone like Stephen R. Covey, who put a spotlight on the rich value of blending different viewpoints to forge new solutions. In *The Seven Habits of Highly Effective People*, Covey (2013) asserts that innovative solutions proposed by the minds of many are greater than results produced by each of us separately. This isn't just collaboration for the sake of it; this is collaboration as the engine of innovation and progress.

Furthermore, research consistently demonstrates the tangible benefits of such collective efforts on our students' learning journeys. When special and general education teachers collaborate effectively, there's a noticeable elevation in teacher effectiveness; this directly leads our students who are compromised by our traditional education models to experience improved academic and social experiences and outcomes (Huberman et al., 2012; Murawski & Lee Swanson, 2001). This evidence supports the idea that collective pedagogy is not only a strategy for professional development but a foundational element for fostering inclusive environments where all students can thrive. In this chapter, we will explore the transformative power of collective pedagogy through co-teaching and co-planning.

Co-Teaching: Collaborating Through Collective Pedagogy

When we think about ways to collaboratively support our special education teachers, one approach that deserves sincere consideration is *co-teaching*—a collective pedagogical effort where two educators work together to facilitate learning for the same group of students. Co-teaching is a popular collaborative model that aims to support students with disabilities in receiving equitable access to and instruction from general education curriculum (Cook & McDuffie-Landrum, 2020). Now, you might be thinking, "We can't possibly make room for co-teaching in our school schedule"; or perhaps you've tried it before and felt it wasn't the right fit; or you're currently implementing this practice in your schools and want to consider its effectiveness. If you're reading this section with excitement, you may have already seen the positive impact of co-teaching or are eager to explore it further. Regardless of your previous experience, let me share my perspective with you. The beauty of co-teaching is that you can customize it to suit your school's unique needs. The possibilities are endless!

The idea of co-teaching initially gained popularity as a strategy to address inclusive mandates from the Individuals with Disabilities Education Act (2004) and the No Child Left Behind Act (2002). The No Child Left Behind Act was replaced by the Every Student Succeeds Act in 2015, which mandates equitable access to general curriculum for all students (Every Student Succeeds Act, 2015; No Child Left Behind Act, 2002). Through these acts, the U.S. Department of Education encouraged more teacher accountability for student achievement, namely general education teachers (Friend, Cook, Hurley-Chamberlain, & Shamberger, 2010).

There is more to be said here, but that's a conversation for another day. What is essential to take away here is that general and special educators supporting all students together could maximize the amount of time students with disabilities would experience equitable access to general education programming alongside their peers (Willis, Bruno, Scott, & Bateman, 2022). After all, prioritizing collaboration through pedagogy is essential to meeting the needs of most of our diverse learners who deserve specially designed instruction (Konrad et al., 2014), as most of our students with IEPs spend the majority of their school time in what are general education environments.

I conducted a study of sixty-seven general and special educators across nine online schools. My research focus was to study their perspectives on meeting the needs of online learners with learning disabilities. Nearly all (97 percent) of these general and special education teachers perceived that collaboration with one another would inform their instructional practices for meeting the needs of students with learning disabilities (Wall, 2023, 2024). Moreover, Michael Weerts's (2020) research finds that just over 93 percent of in-person general and special education co-teachers indicated co-teaching increased their opportunities to provide differentiated instruction and positively contributed to students' improved learning outcomes (Weerts, 2020).

After co-teaching's initial introduction in education in the early 2000s, further research and practice have increasingly revealed its significant positive impact on both teacher and student outcomes (Friend, 2018; Wexler et al., 2018; Wilkins, 2022). Marilyn Friend (2018), an educator and researcher known for groundbreaking work on co-teaching, emphasizes the limitless potential of co-teaching in contributing to improved academic achievement for all students. This powerful partnership leverages the collaborative expertise of at least two teachers to enhance instructional plans, resulting in remarkable benefits.

Research findings support the advantages of co-teaching across diverse educational settings. For instance, studies on co-taught elementary classes (Friend, 2018; Murawski, 2010) consistently demonstrate higher academic achievement compared to classes in which students with disabilities receive specially designed instruction outside of general education classes. This trend holds true for students in grades 1–10 (Friend, 2018). I've had the pleasure of studying a fifth-grade classroom co-taught by Jorge (J) and Amanda in the Upland Unified School District whose students' state assessment scores exceed their schoolwide performance. The empirical evidence reinforces the positive impact of co-teaching, showing improved academic achievement (Crouse et al., 2018; Tahir, Doelger, & Hynes, 2019; Weerts, 2020).

Qualitative studies further highlight the value and effectiveness of co-teaching (King-Sears, Jenkins, & Brawand, 2020; Prizeman, 2021). It is important to note there is a need for continued research. When considering implementation of one or more co-teaching models—which I describe further in the following sections—you might consider devising an action research plan or a Plan-Do-Study-Act cycle to effectively plan and assess your implementation (Lewis, 2015). Furthermore, the design, implementation, and effectiveness of co-teaching in online schools, beyond the COVID-19 pandemic, has been understudied. I look forward to the future of this research.

The focus of this chapter is primarily on equipping school leaders in implementing and overseeing co-teaching and co-planning between general and special educators. Still, it's important to recognize that the principles I discuss here have broader applicability. The benefits of collective pedagogy, as I explore in this chapter, can extend to other programs and support structures within your educational institution, enriching the experiences of both students and staff. Furthermore, it is always important to consider the unique needs of your online, hybrid, or brick-and-mortar school environment.

Attributes of an Effective Co-Teaching Model

Co-teaching is, at its core, a collaborative endeavor that brings together two educators to jointly facilitate learning for the same group of students. As educational leaders, your role is pivotal in implementing and ensuring the success of this strategy within your institution. As I discussed earlier, co-teaching can manifest in various forms, and it's crucial to understand that merely having two teachers in the same physical or virtual space doesn't guarantee its effectiveness. To ensure the best outcomes, it's imperative to incorporate key characteristics into your co-teaching model. In the following list, I highlight eight critical attributes, always keeping in mind that co-teaching is an instructional strategy that you should tailor to meet the unique needs and context of your school. As educational leaders, you serve as the architects, facilitators, and overseers of co-teaching within your school community, and your guidance plays a central role in determining its impact.

What truly makes the difference are the specific characteristics and strategies that contribute to the effectiveness of co-teaching.

1. **Leadership expertise:** Many school leaders possess the knowledge, skills, and beliefs necessary to plan, support, and oversee co-teaching effectively and collaboratively. To strengthen your expertise, you and your team can do the following.
    - Participate in professional learning focused on co-teaching frameworks and inclusive instructional practices.
    - Collaborate with experienced co-teachers to observe best practices and understand partnership dynamics.
    - Develop coaching skills to provide constructive feedback to co-teaching teams.

2. **Stakeholder engagement:** Meaningful communication with stakeholders is crucial for garnering support for co-teaching initiatives. You and your team can do the following to facilitate dialogue with stakeholders.
    - Host informational sessions to explain the benefits of co-teaching and provide stakeholders with opportunities to share input and feedback.
    - Conduct surveys or focus groups to identify concerns and build trust with teachers, parents, and community members.
    - Partner with parent-teacher organizations or local education advocates to amplify the impact of co-teaching initiatives.

3. **Resource availability:** Be careful to consider adequate resources, including classroom space (whether physical or virtual), materials, technology, and planning time, as these are some of the essential resources of co-teaching. To ensure useful resources are readily available, you and your team can do the following.
    - Allocate a budget for technology and tools that support co-teaching, potentially including platforms for virtual collaboration.
    - Ensure planning spaces are equipped to meet the needs of co-teaching teams, whether for in-person or virtual classrooms.

- Regularly review resource use and address gaps proactively to ensure co-teaching teams have what they need.

4. **Teacher preparedness:** Professional learning, as we discussed in chapter 2 (page 37), is key and necessary to ensure teachers are equipped for equitable contributions to co-teaching (Chitiyo & Brinda, 2018). You and your team can do the following to support teacher preparation.

    - Provide training on co-teaching models, Universal Design for Learning (UDL; CAST, n.d.), and collaborative problem solving. *UDL* is a framework developed by CAST (n.d.) that is designed to optimize teaching and learning for all students by providing multiple means of engagement, representation, and expression. This approach emphasizes the importance of designing lessons that are flexible and accessible, meeting the diverse needs of learners. In the context of co-teaching, UDL provides a shared framework for general and special education teachers to collaboratively create inclusive learning experiences, ensuring all students can access, participate in, and succeed in the classroom.

    - Establish peer coaching systems where experienced co-teachers mentor new teams. Be sure to circle back to chapter 1 (page 7) of this book if necessary.

    - Use tools like video reflections to help teachers analyze and refine their practices.

5. **Collaborative culture:** A strong sense of belonging fosters collective pedagogy for educators and students alike (Strogilos & King-Sears, 2019). To cultivate this culture, you and your team can do the following.

    - Organize regular team meetings to encourage idea sharing, discussion, and mutual problem solving.

    - Create communities of practice where co-teachers can provide feedback, ask questions, and share resources.

    - Walk the walk. Lead by example by participating in collaborative activities and modeling inclusive leadership practices.

6. **Dedicated planning time:** Schedule time for collaborative planning and data analysis, as these are essential for successful co-teaching (Friend, 2018). To incorporate dedicated collaboration time, you and your team can do the following.
    - Include shared planning time in the master schedule to ensure consistency.
    - Offer creative solutions such as extended planning periods, early-release days, or flexible scheduling to support co-teachers.
    - Encourage teams to use their planning time to align goals, analyze student progress, and design inclusive lesson plans.
7. **Ongoing program evaluation:** A systematic approach to evaluation supports continuous improvement. We discussed this critical component of a successful program in chapter 2 (page 37). Here is how you can address this essential component with your team.
    - Implement program evaluation plans that include student feedback, data analysis, and teacher reflections.
    - Review student outcomes regularly to assess the effectiveness of co-teaching on academic and social-emotional growth.
    - Facilitate quarterly review sessions with co-teaching teams to reflect on successes, identify challenges, and plan next steps.
8. **Celebrations of success:** Recognition of effort and success positively contributes to school culture and teacher satisfaction (Henderson, 2014; Muhammad, 2018). To build a culture of celebration, you and your team can do the following.
    - Highlight co-teaching achievements in newsletters, staff meetings, and schoolwide events.
    - Create awards or certificates to celebrate milestones such as innovative teaching strategies or student progress goals.
    - Invite co-teaching teams to share their success stories to inspire others and reinforce a positive culture of collaboration.

By integrating these attributes into their co-teaching model, educators can transform this instructional strategy into a powerful tool. Moreover, when teachers experience success and satisfaction in the co-teaching environment, it has a positive ripple effect on the entire school culture. I've had the privilege of hearing this directly from staff. In essence, co-teaching, when infused with these essential elements, becomes a dynamic and impactful approach to education, capable of achieving its full potential. At the end of the chapter, you'll find co-teaching resources in the Takeaway Tool Kit (page 83) that can aid in your team's reflection and planning processes.

Common Co-Teaching Models

As we dive deeper into the dynamics of co-teaching, it's fundamental to understand the different models through which this collective pedagogy can manifest. Each model offers distinct advantages and considerations tailored to the varied needs and contexts of the classroom environment. By understanding the core tenets of these models, school leaders, in partnership with their teachers, can make informed decisions about which approach best aligns with their instructional goals and school needs. The following are the five co-teaching models predominantly discussed and considered in education around the world.

One Teach, One Assist

The *one teach, one assist* approach typically involves one teacher leading the lesson while the assisting teacher provides targeted support where necessary (Cook & McDuffie-Landrum, 2020; Friend & Barron, 2022). Roles might alternate based on lesson elements such as subject matter, student needs, teachers' preferences and strengths, and so on. In an online school, this approach might involve one teacher delivering the lesson through a virtual platform while the assisting teacher moderates the chat for questions, provides links or imagery resources that support accessibility, or provides individualized help through private messages. In a brick-and-mortar classroom, the assisting teacher might circulate among students to offer one-on-one support or manage small-group activities while the lead teacher conducts the main lesson.

The effectiveness of this model hinges significantly on the active involvement of both educators. It's crucial that assisting teachers are not relegated to the sidelines but rather are fully engaged in the teaching process. This active collaboration aims to ensure the co-teaching partnership leverages its full potential so that it not only benefits the students but enhances the teaching dynamics as well. As outlined by Chris A. Sweigart and Timothy J. Landrum (2015) and reiterated by Marilyn Friend and Tammy Barron (2022), a passive stance from the assisting teacher could diminish the co-teaching model's effectiveness, and I've witnessed this firsthand! Thus, ensuring an equitable partnership and a shared distribution of responsibilities is vital for sustaining this model's success.

What might this look like in the classroom? Here's an example. In the one teach, one assist co-teaching model, Mr. Valenzuela, a general education teacher, collaborates with Ms. Jones, a special education teacher, in a diverse fourth-grade classroom. Both educators actively engage with all students. Mr. Valenzuela leads core curriculum delivery, providing clear explanations and interactive lessons. Ms. Jones offers individualized support, adjusting instruction as needed. In an online classroom, she provides additional guidance via chat, and in person she circulates for targeted assistance. This flexible approach allows them to adapt to student needs. For instance, Ms. Jones assists with mathematics, and Mr. Valenzuela provides reading support. They also address IEP goals as applicable.

Station Teaching

The *station teaching* model transforms traditional classrooms into vibrant learning environments by creating stations that cater to the diversity of the learners. This method allows students to rotate through stations and engage with a variety of content. In online settings, this approach adapts by using breakout rooms or encouraging students to move to different spaces at home for certain learning activities. At the heart of station teaching is differentiation, which enables teachers to address individual needs through direct instruction, interactive activities, and personalized support.

By redefining the classroom space as a network of interactive learning spaces, station teaching fosters a dynamic, inclusive, and personalized educational journey. It empowers teachers to fulfill multiple roles—from guiding to facilitating to supporting—thus aiming to ensure every student's learning needs are met. What might this look like in the classroom? Here's an example. Mrs. Johnson, a general education teacher, and Mr. Martinez, a special education teacher, implement a versatile station-style co-teaching approach for diverse learners. Their stations are as follows.

- **Independent learning station:** Students engage in independent learning tasks with clear instructions and access to digital resources like interactive math games or self-paced learning modules on a learning management system, promoting self-directed learning.

- **Small-group instruction station:** Mr. Martinez provides targeted mathematics instruction to a small group using manipulatives, imaging, and potentially gaming, adapting to each student's needs. In an online learning environment, Mr. Martinez leads a small-group mathematics session in a virtual breakout room using an online whiteboard and manipulatives like virtual fraction bars or graphing tools to tailor instruction to each student's needs.

- **Peer collaboration station:** Mrs. Johnson facilitates peer collaboration on a science project, fostering relationships and collaboration both online and in person.

- **Technology integration station:** Mr. Martinez supervises a technology station where students explore interactive simulations such as virtual field trips or hands-on digital experiments using platforms like Nearpod (https://nearpod.com) or PhET Interactive Simulations (https://phet.colorado.edu).

- **Creative expression station:** Students express themselves through creative projects to build self-confidence, whether in the classroom or online, by leveraging platforms like digital storyboards, videos, or visual art using tools like Canva (www.canva.com).

Alternative Teaching

Alternative teaching is like having a tag team in the learning environment. For example, the class is split into two squads. One squad huddles, physically or virtually, with the lead teacher for the main lesson, while the other gets some special attention from the co-teacher in a breakout room or other designated physical space, maybe diving deeper into the material or getting a bit of extra help on tricky topics. The beauty of it? Teachers can swap roles so everyone gets a taste of different teaching styles, and every student gets the spotlight at some point. Behind the scenes, our teacher duo is in sync, planning together to make sure the class runs like a well-oiled machine. It's all about making learning inclusive and effective, guaranteeing every student gets their chance to shine.

What might this look like in physical and virtual class spaces? Here are some examples. Mrs. Rodriguez, a general education teacher, and

Mr. Nguyen, a special education teacher, implement the alternative teaching co-teaching model for their diverse learners.

- **Online learning:** Mrs. Rodriguez leads the main lesson online while Mr. Nguyen provides differentiated instruction in virtual breakout sessions for targeted support to ensure personalized guidance for online learners. The groups switch at some point during the session. Another option would be for all students to stay in the main room, and the teachers take turns delivering parts of the instruction.

- **In-person learning:** During in-person learning, Mr. Nguyen leads the core content using engaging strategies while Mrs. Rodriguez supports a smaller group with individualized assistance to reinforce concepts for in-person students. Another option would be for all students to remain together, and the teachers take turns delivering parts of the instruction.

Team Teaching

Team teaching—or, as I like to call it, the *dynamic duo approach*—is all about co-teachers joining forces to conquer the classroom, whether it's online or face-to-face. This approach involves both teachers actively engaging in the facilitation of learning, often alternating roles such as presenting content, facilitating discussions, or supporting student engagement. Think of it as your favorite buddy cop movie but in an educational setting. They've got the flexibility to tag in and out, ensuring that every lesson hits the mark for inclusiveness and fairness, regardless of whether students are in the classroom or online.

What might this look like in your classroom learning space? Here are some examples. Ms. Brown, a general education teacher, and Mr. Welch, a special education teacher, implement team teaching for diverse learners.

- **Online learning:** Ms. Brown and Mr. Welch co-host virtual live sessions, jointly presenting the core curriculum. They facilitate student participation and collaborative learning in an inclusive online environment.

- **In-person learning:** In the classroom, both educators lead the class, engaging students through discussions, hands-on activities, and cooperative learning experiences. This collaborative model ensures an integrated and inclusive educational experience for in-person learners.

One Teach, One Observe

The *one teach, one observe* method is a team effort where one teacher takes the spotlight to teach while the other plays detective, keeping an eye on how students are catching on. This setup is all about gathering clues on student learning in real time, paving the way for smarter teaching moves that hit the mark for every student in the room.

What might this look like in your class space? Here are some examples. Mr. Lewis, the general education teacher, and Mr. Foster, the special educator, implement the one teach, one observe co-teaching model.

- **Online learning:** In the online environment, Mr. Lewis leads the lesson while Mr. Foster observes students' participation and understanding. His observations inform subsequent instruction and support strategies, ensuring focused co-teaching for online learners. The teachers may switch roles as well.

- **In-person learning:** During in-person classes, Mr. Lewis leads discussions and activities while Mr. Foster observes students' interactions and engagement. They collaboratively review observations and plan targeted interventions to enrich the in-person learning experience. The teachers may switch roles as well.

In the next section, we will learn more about co-planning.

Co-Planning: Bringing Educators Together to Meet Student Needs

In our journey toward retaining and nurturing special education teachers, co-planning is a critical aspect of collective pedagogy in schools. While often associated with co-teaching, co-planning is a required element in any student's IEP when more than one service provider or instructor is involved. It is the glue that supports the alignment of all IEP team members in delivering the services and supports outlined in the IEP.

In my experience, this is an area where our field still has room for growth. Too often, co-planning is treated as an optional or secondary task rather than a foundational practice. This lack of prioritization can lead to gaps in communication and inconsistencies in implementing IEP goals, ultimately impacting student outcomes. To truly meet the needs of our diverse learners, we must elevate co-planning to the essential status it deserves with dedicated time, resources, and administrative support.

This section will focus specifically on co-planning within the context of co-teaching, exploring how structured and intentional planning between special and general education teachers can birth inclusive lesson plans that address the diverse needs of all students. Still, it's important to note that the strategies I discuss here extend beyond co-teaching and apply to many scenarios where educators must work together to meet the unique needs of their students. Co-planning is a tool for success and important for fostering inclusive learning environments.

Why Co-Planning Matters for Effective Co-Teaching

I propose co-planning as one of the linchpins of a successful co-teaching strategy, especially when focusing on the contributions of special education teachers. Its significance cannot be overstated, as co-planning lays the groundwork for role clarity, aligned strategies, inclusive pedagogy, and impactful instructional delivery. Without it, the collective synergy required for co-teaching risks becoming fragmented. The following points illustrate why co-planning is indispensable to effective co-teaching.

- **Time is essential:** Research consistently highlights the critical role of time in enabling effective co-planning. A study by Weerts (2020) found that 87.6 percent of co-teaching participants either agreed or strongly agreed that insufficient planning time posed a significant challenge. This statistic supports the importance of prioritizing dedicated planning time as a non-negotiable element of co-teaching. Without adequate time, co-teachers are often forced to improvise, which can lead to misaligned strategies and diminished student outcomes.

- **A scholarly consensus:** The necessity of co-planning is well documented in academic literature, which emphasizes its foundational role in successful co-teaching practices. Educational researchers (Chanmugam & Gerlach, 2013; Friend, 2018; Gately & Gately, 2001; Wilkins, 2022; Wilson, 2016) consistently emphasize that co-planning is critical for clarity, organization, and adaptability. Their collective findings highlight that without structured co-planning, lessons lack coherence, teacher roles become unclear, and the ability to meet diverse student needs is compromised.

- **Leadership makes the difference:** Strong leadership is instrumental in embedding co-planning practices. Leaders must not only afford co-teachers sufficient planning time but also provide the tools, training, and supportive environments that make co-planning effective. This includes scheduling dedicated time in master calendars, offering professional learning experiences tailored to co-planning strategies, and fostering a school culture that values collective pedagogy. When leaders champion co-planning as a priority, they set the stage for integrated and impactful teaching that benefits both educators and students.

Co-teaching is akin to a harmonious dance—a seamless blend of strengths, approaches, innovation, and insights to serve diverse learning spaces. Yet, like any well-rehearsed performance, the success of this "dance" hinges on the preparation. Co-planning serves as this preparatory stage, offering educators the space to align their strategies, brainstorm interventions and enrichment, and synchronize their instructional rhythms. When executed with intention and support, co-planning transforms the co-teaching experience into one that is not only rewarding for teachers but also profoundly impactful for students.

How to Foster Effective Co-Planning

This framework is designed to help you refine co-teaching practices and cultivate co-planning that effectively implements IEPs. By leveraging this road map, you can guide your teams toward seamless collaboration, impactful lesson planning, and a cohesive approach to meeting diverse student needs.

- **Collaborating through brainstorming sessions:** Foster diverse teaching ideas and perspectives to enhance lesson planning. The following are some actions you can take to meet this objective.
  - Schedule regular brainstorming sessions (weekly or biweekly) aligned with planning timelines.
  - Create a safe and inclusive environment where all ideas are valued. Use tools like Padlet (https://padlet.com) for anonymous idea sharing.
  - Encourage teachers to come prepared with preliminary ideas while remaining open to collaborative revisions.
- **Aligning instructional goals and objectives:** Ensure a unified teaching direction and coherence in lessons. The following are some actions you can take to meet this objective.

- Use a shared digital lesson-planning template that highlights goals and objectives.
- Facilitate critical discussions among co-teachers to refine objectives for clarity, relevance, and feasibility.
- Employ SMART goal criteria to ensure goals are actionable and effective (Conzemius & O'Neill, 2014).

- **Identifying and addressing student needs:** Cater to individual student needs for an inclusive classroom environment. The following are some actions you can take to meet this objective.
  - Maintain updated student profiles—including IEP details, language proficiencies, and other relevant data—in a shared, secure location.
  - Host regular teacher discussions to share observations about students' evolving needs and adapt strategies accordingly.
  - Incorporate UDL principles to provide multiple means of representation, engagement, and expression (CAST, n.d.).

- **Ensuring accessibility:** Guarantee every student can access, understand, and succeed in learning activities. The following are actions you can take to meet this objective.
  - Provide training on creating differentiated content, focusing on varied presentation methods, activities, and assessments.
  - Encourage co-teachers to share differentiated materials during planning sessions for peer feedback and refinement.
  - Invest in tools and resources such as screen readers, graphic organizers, or translation apps to support accessibility for all learners.

- **Defining roles and responsibilities:** Clarify roles to ensure effective collaboration and delivery. The following are actions you can take to meet this objective.
  - Develop a co-teaching agreement at the start of the co-teaching partnership period that outlines each teacher's roles, classroom management strategies, and teaching preferences.
  - Schedule regular check-ins to reflect on roles and adjust based on lesson requirements or teacher strengths.

- Empower teachers to take ownership of their roles while providing leadership support as needed.
- **Seeking feedback and continuous improvement:** Refine co-planning processes through consistent feedback and reflection. The following are actions you can take to meet this objective.
  - Establish feedback channels.
    - Facilitate peer observations followed by constructive debriefs.
    - Use student feedback surveys to assess lesson effectiveness from their perspective.
    - Schedule post-lesson reflections for co-teachers to discuss strengths and areas for improvement.
  - Document and review feedback.
    - Use a feedback log or collaborative digital platform to track observations and suggestions.
    - Revisit feedback logs during planning sessions to align future strategies with insights gained.
  - Set feedback expectations.
    - Host a workshop series or share resources on giving and receiving constructive feedback.
    - Encourage timely, specific, and actionable feedback to support meaningful adjustments.
  - Adapt based on feedback.
    - Use insights to tweak co-planning processes, instructional strategies, or resource allocations.
    - If patterns of challenges emerge, organize targeted training sessions to address recurring issues.

This blueprint for effective co-planning provides both a strategic and actionable approach for educational leaders. By guiding co-teachers to align goals, meet diverse student needs, and refine their collaborative practices, it aims to ensure co-planning becomes a seamless, integrated part of your school's culture. Whether your goal is to enhance co-teaching effectiveness or implement IEPs more robustly, this framework serves as a practical tool for fostering collective pedagogy and achieving educational excellence.

Tips From the Top

As we navigate this collaborative path, we often encounter obstacles that can hinder our progress. From communication breakdowns and scheduling conflicts to differences in teaching philosophies and the need for more targeted training, each barrier presents an opportunity for growth and improvement. This section is dedicated to identifying these common challenges and providing practical, actionable insights to help you, as a school leader, facilitate smoother collective pedagogy among your teaching staff.

- **Foster clear communication.**
    - Schedule regular, dedicated meetings to align co-teachers and foster active listening and mutual understanding.
    - Leverage collaborative tools like shared calendars, messaging platforms, and digital whiteboards to streamline communication.
- **Address time constraints.**
    - Carve out non-negotiable weekly co-planning times in the master schedule.
    - Integrate co-planning into existing professional development sessions or staff meetings to maximize time efficiency.
- **Bridge teaching philosophy differences.**
    - Facilitate mutual respect and collaboration through workshops or structured discussions focused on blending teaching styles.
    - Encourage co-teachers to co-design lesson plans, leveraging each other's strengths for a unified classroom approach.
- **Clarify responsibilities.**
    - Define and document clear roles and responsibilities for each co-teacher to avoid confusion and overlap.
    - Conduct regular reflective meetings for co-teachers to provide feedback, share insights, and adjust responsibilities as needed.
- **Provide targeted training.**
    - Offer professional development sessions that focus on collaborative teaching strategies and the needs of diverse learners.

- Encourage co-teachers to attend training together to ensure alignment in approach and expectations.
- **Ensure resource availability.**
  - Create a shared repository for lesson plans, materials, and resources to simplify access and collaboration.
  - Optimize physical and virtual spaces to support co-teaching, reconfiguring as necessary to meet team needs.

Voices From the Field

The following vignettes bring together firsthand accounts from educators who have embraced the challenges and rewards of co-teaching and co-planning. Collective pedagogy, when thoughtfully implemented, has the potential to transform classrooms into inclusive, dynamic environments where all students can thrive. These stories provide practical insights, innovative strategies, and candid reflections on the partnerships that make co-teaching successful. They highlight the importance of collaboration, communication, and shared commitment to student growth—principles that lie at the heart of this chapter.

Each story is unique, showcasing the distinct ways educators navigate co-teaching to create meaningful learning experiences. Jorge "Mr. J" Gonzalez and Amanda Soto share how their intentional approach to team teaching and their "enlarge the end zone" philosophy redefine success in their inclusive classroom. Meanwhile, Ariel Baird recounts her partnership with a high school mathematics teacher, demonstrating the power of preparation, open communication, and shared responsibility in fostering an effective co-teaching dynamic.

ENLARGING THE END ZONE: A CO-TEACHING PHILOSOPHY

Co-teaching can take many forms, but we have been very thoughtful about the models we use. Our go-to model is often team teaching. This model choice is purposeful for us because we care deeply about modeling academic discourse, appropriate interaction, and different ways of thinking. In this way, students see their teachers not only teach the content but interact in a way that models positive interaction for them. We have thought deeply about the qualities we want to foster in our students. Our ultimate goal is to nurture our students to be successful not only academically but interpersonally.

Our co-teaching strategy goes beyond the classroom. We believe that we can make a cohesive, inclusive educational setting with our enlarge the end zone theory. In typical classrooms, students "score" when they get an academic win. Well, if that's the only way students can score, then if we're honest, our students with disabilities will hardly, if ever, score. Enlarge your end zone! So, in our classroom, our content is not solely academics. We teach interpersonal skills and life skills; we give responsibility grades; we teach manners. We even teach kids how to swim! We are intentional about what we give points to in our classroom. When we do this, we find that (1) general education students and students with disabilities score more equally; (2) students with disabilities are often very good at the other skills we teach; and (3) all our students feel rigor and a sense of accomplishment.

A *successful* co-teaching team is definitely not ever a *perfect* co-teaching team. We came into our co-teaching partnership with a dedication to having open and often difficult conversations about our teaching philosophies and how to meet student needs. In the beginning, we sat down together and chatted about each of our non-negotiables. For one of us, it was a deep desire for students to have routine and high expectations. For the other, it was a desire for students to feel at home and part of a strong classroom and school community. Together, we were able to meld these often-perceived-opposite philosophies to create a cohesive learning community where every student has an opportunity to thrive, achieve, and feel success.

—Jorge "Mr. J" Gonzalez, Education Specialist (co-teacher), California, and Amanda Soto, General Subjects Educator (co-teacher), California

LESSONS FROM A CO-TEACHING TEAM

Teaching between a high school content teacher and a special education teacher can vary significantly depending on personalities, training, and planning. I worked as a special education co-teacher in a Title I high school, partnering with various teachers across core subjects. Each experience was unique, and by the time I was assigned to co-teach Mathematics 1, I had a clear understanding of my strengths and strategies to support my students.

I met Jill, my new co-teacher, and we quickly discovered our similar personalities and teaching philosophies. We decided to "leave our egos at the door" and prioritize open communication and collaboration. Despite my initial worries about my mathematics ability, Jill's willingness to support and guide me helped us form a strong partnership. We shared responsibilities equally, from grading to planning lessons, and ensured both our names were on the classroom door and syllabus, emphasizing our co-teaching role.

Throughout the summer, I studied the Mathematics 1 curriculum, and Jill and I exchanged ideas and strategies. This preparation paid off immensely. We entered the new school year with a solid plan, tailored activities, and a commitment to support each other and our students. This collaboration made our co-teaching experience the most effective and rewarding one I've had.

—Ariel Baird, Special Education Teacher, Kansas

 Takeaway Tool Kit

As we conclude this chapter, let me introduce some carefully curated tools designed to support you in leading co-teaching and co-planning initiatives. These resources are tailored to enhance co-teaching practices within your unique school environment. Whether your teaching teams are exploring co-teaching for the first time or aiming to refine their collaborative strategies, these tools are invaluable resources. They provide a structured yet flexible road map, guiding educators toward a harmonious and impactful co-teaching experience that benefits every student.

Figure 3.1 (page 84) will help you with preplanning, and you can complete it alone or collaboratively. If you're at the starting line wondering how to kick things off, this is the tool for you. It walks you through everything from the big-picture benefits of co-teaching, especially for special education, down to the nitty-gritty of getting it off the ground. This is your pregame strategy session, designed to make sure you and your teachers are on the same page and are ready to hit the ground running.

Figure 3.2 (page 85) presents reflection questions for equitable co-planning. You can use these alone or collaboratively. Think of these questions as your compass: They're going to guide you through evaluating how co-planning is going at your school. It's all about taking a hard look at what's working, what's not, and where you can celebrate or tweak things. This is your chance to really dig deep and make sure that your collaborative efforts are as strong and effective as they can be.

Job Satisfaction and Professional Growth
How can co-teaching enhance job satisfaction for special education teachers?

How can co-teaching foster professional growth for these teachers?

What training can we provide to support this transition?

Challenges and Collaboration Opportunities
What challenges do our special education teachers face that co-teaching can address?

How does co-teaching open avenues for collaboration with general education peers?

Student Needs and Vision Alignment
How does co-teaching better address specific student needs?

How does it align with our broader vision for inclusive education?

Co-Teaching Introduction
How should we introduce co-teaching to our staff?

How can we assess their readiness for co-teaching?

How can we gauge their interest in this approach?

Resources and Communication
Which existing resources can aid our transition into co-teaching?

How will we effectively communicate its advantages to all stakeholders?

Figure 3.1: Reflection questions when considering co-teaching for the first time.
*Visit **go.SolutionTree.com/specialneeds** for a free reproducible version of this figure.*

Foundations and Culture of Co-Planning
How are we prioritizing and carving out dedicated time for co-planning in our school's schedule?

Are teachers actively engaged in co-planning sessions and ensuring alignment in curriculum, instructional strategies, and student accommodations?

How can we foster a culture of mutual respect and shared purpose during co-planning sessions?

What training or professional development opportunities can we offer to enhance the effectiveness of co-planning?

Implementation and Alignment
How do we ensure that co-planned lessons are not only aligned with curriculum but also tailored to address the unique needs of all students, especially those in special education?

Are there opportunities for interdisciplinary projects or units that promote curriculum alignment and foster cross-department collaboration?

Resources and Tools
What tools, templates, or collaborative platforms can be streamlined to enhance the co-planning process?

Feedback and Refinement
How are we facilitating feedback and adjustments in the co-planning process to continuously refine and improve?

In what ways are we recognizing and celebrating the successes that emerge from effective co-planning?

Figure 3.2: Reflection questions for equitable co-planning.

*Visit **go.SolutionTree.com/specialneeds** for a free reproducible version of this figure.*

For those of you who've already started on this journey, figure 3.3 is your next step. This tool is all about taking stock of where you are now.

Integration and Impact Assessment
How well has co-teaching been integrated into our school's instructional practices and culture?

What data can we gather to assess the impact of co-teaching on student outcomes, teacher satisfaction, and school culture?

Are there specific co-teaching models that have been particularly successful in our context?

Challenges, Feedback, and Refinement
What challenges have emerged since the initiation of co-teaching?

How do we consistently gather feedback from teachers, students, and parents on their co-teaching experiences?

How can we adapt and improve our co-teaching practices to better serve our students and staff?

Peer Learning and Best Practices
What avenues exist for peer observation and sharing of insights among co-teaching pairs?

How can we further encourage the sharing of co-teaching best practices within our institution?

Recognition, Benefits, and Future Planning
How are we celebrating the achievements of our co-teaching teams?

In what ways is co-teaching benefiting our special education teachers specifically?

What future goals or plans should we consider continuing to support co-teaching success?

Figure 3.3: Reflection questions for co-teaching implementation.
*Visit **go.SolutionTree.com/specialneeds** for a free reproducible version of this figure.*

It's a chance to celebrate the wins, big and small, and to pinpoint where you might need to pivot or push harder. This is about making sure that co-teaching isn't just happening—it's thriving and growing in your school.

Figure 3.4 (page 88) and figure 3.5 (page 90) are essential tools meticulously designed to bolster your teachers' collective pedagogy. Together, they offer a comprehensive suite to navigate the complexities of co-teaching, from initial planning stages to post-lesson reflections.

The action checklist (figure 3.4) is an in-depth guide for teacher teams detailing critical focus areas such as lesson planning, instructional strategy adaptation, and reflective teaching outcomes. It encourages collaborative preparation, underscores continuous professional development, and advocates for adaptable teaching methods that promote an inclusive learning environment. By adhering to the action points outlined, educators can enhance their cooperative teaching methods, ensuring both teachers leverage their strengths to the fullest while fostering an atmosphere of continuous improvement.

Complementing the action checklist, the planning template in figure 3.5 (page 90) provides a structured framework that streamlines the co-teaching process. It enables educators to collaboratively design and implement lessons, ensuring clear communication and an equitable distribution of responsibilities. This forward-thinking approach not only aligns with a shared vision for student success but also facilitates a thorough examination of each lesson's impact, laying the groundwork for effective and reflective teaching practices.

I want you to see these tools as more than just worksheets or checklists; they're a way for you to shape and sharpen the co-teaching experience, making it as impactful and fulfilling as possible for everyone involved—teachers, students, and, yes, you, too. Each tool is a conversation starter, a way to bring you and your teachers closer, working hand in hand toward a common goal. So, take these tools, tailor them to your needs, and let's make co-teaching in your school not just a possibility but a resounding success.

Teacher Name: _____   Date: _____

Topic	Checklist	Action Notes
Co-Planning and Preparation	☐ Collectively plan lessons with your co-teacher, considering differentiated instruction and accommodations. ☐ Clearly define the roles and responsibilities of each co-teacher for the upcoming lessons. ☐ Set specific learning objectives and goals for student outcomes. ☐ Share resources, materials, and technology needed for the lesson.	
Professional Learning and Collaboration	☐ Identify areas where additional training or support is needed (such as content knowledge or collaboration skills). ☐ Attend relevant professional development workshops or training sessions. ☐ Participate in collaborative meetings with your co-teacher to discuss lesson plans, objectives, and student progress. ☐ Seek feedback from your co-teacher and provide constructive input to improve co-teaching practices.	
Classroom Setup and Resources	☐ Ensure the classroom setup is conducive to co-teaching, with adequate space for both teachers and students. ☐ Organize materials and resources to support the lesson, including any assistive technology. ☐ Confirm that students have access to the necessary learning materials, whether online or in person.	
Instructional Strategies	☐ Implement co-teaching strategies based on your chosen model (for example, one teach, one assist; team teaching; station teaching; and so on). ☐ Adapt your teaching approach to meet the diverse needs of all students. ☐ Provide clear instructions and explanations for the class. ☐ Use universal design techniques to address individual needs. ☐ Monitor student engagement and understanding during the lesson.	
Student Support and Differentiation	☐ Address the needs of diverse learners and students with disabilities, ensuring they receive appropriate accommodations and support. ☐ Offer individualized assistance to students who require it, whether in person or online. ☐ Encourage peer collaboration and inclusive interactions among students.	

Assessment and Data Collection	☐ Collect data on student progress and participation during the lesson. ☐ Use assessment results to inform your teaching and adjust as needed. ☐ Collaborate with your co-teacher to review assessment data and plan interventions.
Reflection and Improvement	☐ Engage in post-lesson reflection with your co-teacher to assess the effectiveness of the co-teaching model you used. ☐ Identify areas for improvement and discuss strategies to enhance future co-teaching practices. ☐ Implement changes based on the reflection and feedback process.
Equity and Inclusion	☐ Ensure that co-teaching practices promote equity and inclusion for all students, regardless of their background or abilities. ☐ Advocate for the needs of students with disabilities and diverse learners to create an inclusive learning environment.
Student Outcomes and Well-Being	☐ Continuously monitor student academic progress and social-emotional development. ☐ Provide additional support or modifications for students who require them. ☐ Foster a positive and inclusive classroom culture that supports student well-being.
Team Communication and Collaboration	☐ Maintain open and regular communication with your co-teacher to ensure alignment in teaching strategies and goals. ☐ Collaboratively plan and adjust instructional practices based on student needs and feedback.
Action Plan for Continuous Improvement	☐ Develop an action plan based on the identified areas for refinement. ☐ Set specific goals and timelines for implementing changes in co-teaching practices. ☐ Track progress in achieving the action plan's objectives.

Figure 3.4: Co-teaching action checklist.

Visit go.SolutionTree.com/specialneeds for a free reproducible version of this figure.

Lesson Date: _____

Subject or Topic: _____

Teaching Strategy: _____

Special Education Teacher Responsibilities:

1. _____
2. _____
3. _____

General Education Teacher Responsibilities:

1. _____
2. _____
3. _____

Required Materials:

1. _____
2. _____
3. _____

Assessment Methods (for example, quiz, project, observation):

Post-Lesson Reflection

What went well?

What needs improvement?

Did any accommodations stand out?

Figure 3.5: Co-teaching planning tool.

Visit **go.SolutionTree.com/specialneeds** *for a free reproducible version of this figure.*

Wrap-Up

As we close this chapter, let's recognize the power of collective pedagogy in driving meaningful collaboration through co-teaching and co-planning. These practices are not just strategies—they are truly essential in fostering inclusive learning environments where educators unite their strengths in the art of teaching. By fostering intentional co-teaching partnerships and embedding co-planning into your school's culture, you lay the groundwork for both teacher and student success.

This emphasis on collaboration leads us naturally to the next chapter, where we'll explore the critical process of collaboratively preparing and implementing IEPs.

Chapter Four

Preparing and Implementing Collaborative IEPs

In the world of special education, few documents are as pivotal as the IEP. A well-crafted IEP can be the difference between a student flourishing or becoming lost in a system that fails to address their uniqueness. I expect that many readers who choose to invest time in reading this book understand what an IEP is; however, for those of you who do not, allow me to share a brief overview. An *IEP* is a federally mandated document under the Individuals with Disabilities Education Act (2004) that outlines a tailored educational plan for students with disabilities. It includes key components such as present levels of academic achievement, measurable annual goals, accommodations and modifications, and a description of services to be provided. The IEP serves as a road map for educators, parents, and service providers to collaborate in meeting the unique needs of the student, ensuring access to the general education curriculum and fostering progress toward their educational goals.

The endeavor of crafting and executing an IEP necessitates collaboration, communication, and commitment from an entire team. Each team member—from parents, general education teachers, and special education teachers to specialists and school leaders—plays a distinct and indispensable role. The interconnectedness of these roles emphasizes that while the IEP might be individualized for the student, its success hinges on collective effort.

The act of working together fosters a sense of unity, bridging any potential gaps and aiming for seamless communication and understanding.

As you proceed into this chapter, you'll discover practical tools, strategies, and insights to help you oversee effective program creation, implementation, and continuous development. From understanding the intricacies of IEP creation to adopting an ongoing data-driven mindset, you'll be equipped with the foundational knowledge and tools necessary to cultivate a collaborative environment that champions the uniqueness of every student.

School leaders bear a weighty responsibility in ensuring the IEP is created collaboratively and implemented according to its design. As a school leader, you must oversee, facilitate, and even arbitrate the diverse perspectives that help craft these personalized learning road maps. As these programs take shape and move into the realm of execution, leaders remain guardians of the process, ensuring every aspect of the IEP is brought to life in the classroom and beyond.

In this chapter, we'll explore the multifaceted world of collaborative IEP creation, its execution, and the subsequent *data mining*, a term I adopted from a dear friend and phenomenal education leader, Dr. Shinay Bowman. The harmonious integration of co-planning, co-implementation, and co-analysis is necessary to build a comprehensive program, successfully implement it, and continuously refine it.

Navigating the Complexities of IEPs

Imagine IEPs as lighthouses, guiding the way for educators, community partners, parents, and students alike. These plans, however, are far from straightforward. Navigating the creation and implementation of an IEP involves recognizing the individuality of each student, embracing diverse educational perspectives, and diligently adhering to legal mandates—all while ensuring that the process remains adaptive and responsive to the student's evolving needs. It's a synergy of expertise, law, care, and collaboration.

As we examine co-creating and co-implementing IEPs, let us first develop a shared understanding of the essential elements of an IEP.

- **Multidimensional student profiles:** IEPs are as unique as the students they serve. Educators must consider academic performance, social-emotional needs, medical needs, family dynamics, and more when creating an IEP.
  - *Leader's role*—School leaders should make certain all team members have access to comprehensive student data and

should facilitate collaborative discussions to integrate these insights into a holistic plan. You can also promote and facilitate professional learning experiences on how to understand and address multifaceted student needs.

- **Diverse educational perspectives:** The IEP team is a melting pot of expertise that includes families, general and special education teachers, school psychologists, speech therapists, and other specialists. While this diversity strengthens the plan, it can also present challenges.
  - *Leader's role*—Leaders are facilitators and supervisors of this process, making certain all voices are heard, resolving conflicts when perspectives differ, and guiding the team in aligning their contributions into a coherent and actionable plan. Establishing clear communication protocols and fostering mutual respect are essential actions you can take.
- **Legal and procedural considerations:** IEPs are legally binding documents that must comply with local, state, and federal regulations. From meeting timelines to the specific language used, these procedural elements add layers of complexity.
  - *Leader's role*—Leaders must stay informed about legal requirements and procedural updates and provide training and resources to ensure the team remains compliant. You should also monitor adherence to timelines and oversee the accuracy of documentation to avoid legal pitfalls.
- **Dynamic implementation needs:** The journey doesn't end with a signed IEP—it begins there. Effective implementation requires ongoing monitoring, adjustments, and collaboration to adapt the plan as students' needs evolve.
  - *Leader's role*—School leaders can establish systems for progress monitoring, facilitate regular review discussions, and make certain that teachers and staff have the tools and support they need to implement and adapt the IEP as needed. You should encourage a feedback culture where team members feel comfortable suggesting necessary changes.
- **Family collaboration:** Parents and guardians are crucial allies in the IEP process. Building trust with families, ensuring their

voices are heard, and incorporating their insights into the plan are essential steps.

- *Leader's role*—Leaders should prioritize family engagement by providing opportunities to discuss their children's progress as an ongoing process, and not only at the IEP meeting. You can also foster a welcoming environment during IEP meetings to strengthen parent-school relationships.

Figure 4.1 illustrates the cyclical nature of the IEP meeting process, beginning with the pre-IEP meeting stage, where data gathering, stakeholder engagement, brainstorming, and consolidation of data and insights occur. It then transitions to the post-IEP meeting phase, which involves debriefing, regular check-ins, accommodation prioritization, progress monitoring, and preparation for the subsequent IEP review. The arrows signify the ongoing, iterative approach to refining and enhancing individualized educational programs.

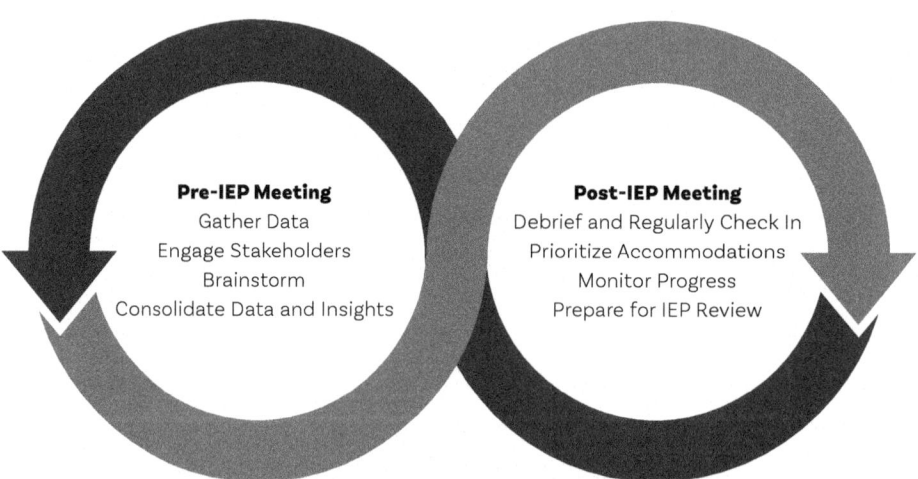

Figure 4.1: A dual-phase approach to optimizing IEP meetings.

A successful IEP process doesn't begin or end with the meeting itself—it's built on the groundwork laid before and the follow-through that comes after. While the meeting itself is undeniably important, this book focuses on the essential pre- and post-IEP phases, as they form the foundation for meaningful collaboration and sustained implementation. For resources or professional development on conducting effective IEP meetings, I encourage you to explore the wealth of existing materials or consider the training sessions I offer as a school partner.

The following sections outline actionable steps for these crucial phases and emphasize the school leader's role in facilitating a seamless and inclusive process. By focusing on collaborative preparation and follow-through, leaders can help ensure that IEPs are not just compliant but transformative for students and educators alike.

Pre-IEP Meeting Steps

Thoughtful preparation sets the stage for a successful IEP meeting. The following pre-meeting steps are designed to create a solid foundation for developing an informed and effective IEP. These steps highlight the importance of collaboration, careful planning, and the use of technology to enhance the educational planning process.

Step 1: Gather Data

Data gathering is a foundational step in the IEP process because it provides a comprehensive understanding of the student's uniqueness, strengths, and areas requiring support. Without accurate and thorough data, the IEP team risks creating a plan that lacks the precision and customization needed to effectively support the student. This step ensures that every decision made during the IEP meeting is grounded in evidence, fostering accountability and alignment with the student's goals.

The types of data leaders should ensure are collected include:

- **Academic performance data,** such as assessment scores, class assignments, progress reports, and strategies and support, to understand the student's current level of achievement
- **Behavioral data,** including observations, applied strategies, and functional behavior assessments, to identify patterns and develop effective support systems
- **Social-emotional data,** which may include teacher and counselor observations and applied strategies or feedback from students and families, to address nonacademic factors influencing learning
- **Specialized data,** such as medical reports, therapy notes, community partner input, or language proficiency assessments, to inform accommodations and supports

- **Feedback from the student, parents, and caregivers,** offering valuable insights into the student's experiences and needs outside of the school environment

By gathering and organizing this diverse range of data, leaders help ensure that the IEP process is informed, inclusive, and actionable. To guarantee successful, collaborative data gathering, leaders can do the following.

- Champion the implementation of unified digital platforms to ensure that all relevant student performance data are centrally housed and easily accessible to those involved in the IEP process.
- Promote regular check-ins among teachers to make certain that data are not only collected but also reviewed and analyzed collaboratively.
- Organize training sessions to empower educators and parents with the skills to discern and make sense of the collected data.
- Emphasize the importance of parent feedback in the data collection phase to reinforce a holistic approach to understanding each student's educational journey.

Step 2: Engage Stakeholders

Stakeholder engagement is a crucial component of the IEP process because it ensures that all voices contributing to the student's success are heard, valued, and integrated into the plan. The term *stakeholder* encompasses a broad range of individuals, including parents or guardians, general and special education teachers, school counselors, speech and occupational therapists, school psychologists, administrators, and even the student. Each stakeholder brings a unique perspective and expertise that enrich the IEP process, so involving each of them ensures the IEP is both comprehensive and actionable.

This step is important because it creates a shared understanding of the student's needs, aligns efforts across disciplines, and fosters a sense of collective responsibility. Engaging stakeholders also builds trust and transparency, particularly with families, whose input provides invaluable insights into the student's experiences beyond the classroom.

School leaders play a pivotal role in equipping special educators and case managers with the strategies and tools they need for meaningful stakeholder involvement. To facilitate effective engagement, here's what you can do.

- **Advocate for the scheduling of well-planned meetings:** Ensure IEP case managers orchestrate timely conversations with their fellow team members. These interactions provide a platform for discussing a student's uniqueness, strengths, and challenges and include valuable insights.

- **Provide standardized tools for consistency and efficiency:** Offer educators resources such as survey templates, family input forms, discussion guides, checklists, and electronic storage platforms. These tools create a unified approach to gathering input from families and other team members. (See the Takeaway Tool Kit, page 111.)

- **Emphasize inclusivity in stakeholder insights:** Highlight the importance of gathering and integrating feedback from all stakeholders, recognizing that each perspective—whether from a parent, a general education teacher, or a speech therapist—adds depth to the IEP process and supports a well-rounded understanding of the student.

- **Celebrate collaborative efforts:** Reinforce the importance of teamwork in developing a robust and inclusive IEP. Acknowledge and value the contributions of every stakeholder, emphasizing how their collective input leads to a plan that addresses every facet of the student's unique needs.

Step 3: Brainstorm

Brainstorming is a critical component of the IEP co-planning process because it allows team members to collaboratively generate ideas for tailoring the plan to meet the student's unique needs. This step focuses on developing creative and actionable strategies for accommodations, instructional modifications, behavioral supports, and service delivery. By engaging in structured brainstorming, the IEP team can explore innovative ways to address challenges, align goals, and see that plans reflect the student's strengths and areas for growth. This is also a great element to consider bringing into an active IEP meeting.

For school leaders, enabling special education teachers and case managers to navigate brainstorming effectively is crucial. Here's what you can do.

- **Provide resources to facilitate brainstorming:** Equip educators with tools such as brainstorming boards, shared digital documents, or online collaboration platforms—for example, Microsoft OneNote (www.onenote.com), Google Workspace (https://workspace.google.com), or Padlet (https://padlet.com)—to enable the fluid exchange of ideas among team members.

- **Host professional learning experiences:** In chapter 2 (page 37), we discussed the critical importance of professional learning. You might consider including brainstorming in your professional learning plans. For example, consider training that will introduce your team to effective brainstorming techniques, such as mind mapping, the SCAMPER (Substitute, Combine, Adapt, Modify, Put to Another Use, Eliminate, Reverse) method, or rapid ideation. These techniques ensure that brainstorming sessions remain focused and productive.

- **Encourage specific focus areas:** Guide teams in brainstorming strategies and solutions related to key areas such as classroom accommodations, inclusive instructional practices, or approaches to achieving IEP goals. For example, ask the following questions.
    - How can we modify this assignment to ensure accessibility?
    - What tools or resources could enhance the student's engagement?
    - What have we already tried, and how effective were those strategies?

- **Create consistent feedback channels:** Allow educators to share challenges and ideas for improving the brainstorming process. Feedback loops ensure sessions are refined over time and that teachers' voices are valued.

- **Foster an open, innovative environment:** Cultivate a culture where all ideas are welcomed without judgment, aiming to ensure that team members feel their insights are integral to the process. This openness encourages creative solutions and strengthens collaboration.

Step 4: Consolidate Data and Insights

IEP preparation hinges on the ability to synthesize and organize the data and insights gathered in step 1 into a cohesive and actionable format. Case managers are all too familiar with this phase, as consolidation is a necessary part of preparing for the meeting. Consolidating data ensures that all relevant information is integrated into a comprehensive plan that effectively guides the IEP discussion. By aligning data with clear objectives and strategies, the team can collaboratively address the student's unique needs and goals.

As school leaders, it's essential to provide the tools, guidance, and structure necessary to support this process. To facilitate effective consolidation, leaders can do the following.

- **Leverage technology:** Promote the use of digital platforms like Trello (https://trello.com), Google Workspace (https://workspace.google.com), Padlet (https://padlet.com), Evernote (https://evernote.com), or Microsoft Office suites (www.microsoft.com/en-ms/store/collections/officesuites) to organize and merge collected data, feedback, and observations seamlessly. These tools allow team members to collaborate in real time and ensure all voices are represented.

- **Advocate for structured methodologies:** Establish clear protocols for consolidating information, emphasizing the importance of presenting a comprehensive overview of the student's needs, objectives, and strategies.

- **Facilitate regular review meetings:** Schedule quarterly meetings where educators can present and discuss their consolidated findings. These sessions ensure alignment among stakeholders, offer opportunities for refining data, and provide a forum for enhancing teaching practices.

- **Emphasize thorough preparation:** Reinforce the idea that a well-prepared consolidation process is the backbone of an effective IEP discussion. Leaders should encourage attention to detail and provide training to ensure all team members understand the importance of this step.

With the pre-IEP steps laying the groundwork for a collaborative and informed meeting, the process doesn't end once the IEP is developed. The real work begins after the meeting, as implementation and ongoing adjustments determine the plan's success. Post-meeting actions are essential to ensuring that the IEP remains a living document—one that evolves with the student's needs and continues to drive meaningful progress.

Post-IEP Meeting Steps

The steps taken after an IEP meeting play a pivotal role in bringing the plan to life and adapting it to meet the student's unique and evolving needs. These steps sustain momentum and keep the educational strategies outlined in the plan relevant and impactful. The following post-meeting steps focus on monitoring progress and making timely adjustments to ensure the IEP remains a dynamic tool for student success.

Step 1: Debrief and Regularly Check In

Here are several foundational actions school leaders should consider for facilitating effective debriefing and consistent check-ins.

- **Encourage debrief sessions soon after the IEP meeting:** Urge special education case managers to spearhead a structured debrief session within one to ten days following the IEP meeting. This session serves to reinforce a common understanding of the IEP's goals and a clear delineation of each team member's role in its execution. This might also look like the case manager following up with team members via phone, hosting a quick fifteen-minute in-person or virtual meeting, or leveraging electronic platforms or instant chat formats to ensure team members understand their role in implementation.

- **Accentuate the importance of routine check-ins:** Whether they're weekly, biweekly, or monthly, these touchpoints are essential to assess the IEP's ongoing effectiveness, identify potential challenges, and make necessary modifications. We don't want to wait until the common annual renewal date to check in with team members. You might consider leveraging progress reporting time as a check-in time.

- **Advocate for digital platforms for check-in facilitation:** Digital tools that allow for real-time tracking and feedback can be invaluable, keeping everyone in the loop regarding the student's progress.

- **Emphasize the role of adaptability:** While an IEP sets forth a plan, it's pivotal to recognize and adapt to the dynamic needs of the student to ensure their growth and well-being remain central.

Step 2: Prioritize Accommodations

Accommodations are the linchpin in the IEP process as one method for providing tailored support for students to access and meaningfully engage in learning. Successful prioritization and implementation of these accommodations are essential for creating an inclusive learning environment. This topic is especially important to address with general educators for students who participate in general learning environments. Here are some practices you can adopt to emphasize the significance of these accommodations.

- **Clarify the significance of accommodations:** Reinforce the understanding that accommodations are more than just mandated requirements—they break down barriers and enhance accessibility. They are specialized tools designed to bridge learning gaps of all learners and facilitate a student's ability to engage, comprehend, and excel. Thus, every accommodation is essential and must be implemented thoughtfully.

- **Elucidate the nuances of different accommodations:** Facilitate professional learning sessions—and provide ongoing support where necessary—that address the distinctions of different accommodations. These sessions can educate staff on the rationale, proper implementation, and potential challenges associated with each accommodation.

- **Prioritize collaboration among all teachers:** Champion a collaborative approach where special education teachers collaborate closely with other content teachers to ensure seamless integration of accommodations in classroom settings. This is where co-planning comes into play! Reflect on chapter 3 (page 63) and make connections to how co-planning might be relevant, even when students are being co-taught. Special education teachers, service providers, special subjects teachers, and general educators can leverage check-in time to collectively plan how they will support students through their IEP guidelines.

- **Advocate for ongoing monitoring and reflection:** Encourage all teachers to assess the effectiveness of the accommodations in real time, adjusting and refining as necessary to meet the student's evolving needs.

- **Institute and maintain open communication:** Establish open channels of communication between IEP team members. This fosters a space where educators can share insights, offer mutual support, and problem-solve together, ensuring they always tailor accommodations to provide the best support.

Step 3: Monitor Progress

Supporting the continuous growth and success of a student's IEP requires an intricate progress-monitoring system. Here's a strategic approach to guide leaders in the implementation of this critical aspect of the special education process.

- **Emphasize the significance of regular monitoring:** Begin by highlighting that it's not just a legal obligation but a means to ensure every student's learning journey is on the right track. Then, inspect what you expect!
- **Introduce educators to progress-monitoring tools:** Digital platforms, assessment methods, or data-tracking techniques can streamline the progress-monitoring process and offer a centralized location for all pertinent information. Teachers can leverage tools such as iTrack (https://itracktwc.com) for a centralized electronic space to track data and make information accessible to collaborative teams.
- **Champion the importance of interdisciplinary collaboration:** Encourage regular communication among all professionals involved so that insights from different perspectives—such as academic performance, behavioral data, and therapeutic supports—are integrated seamlessly.
- **Organize training sessions on the nuances of progress monitoring:** These sessions could involve workshops on how to effectively use specific tools, interpret data, or address challenges that might emerge during the monitoring process.
- **Implement a channel for feedback:** This allows special education case managers to consistently share the student's progress, which can be discussed during regular check-ins.
- **Promote the value of reflective practices:** By routinely reviewing and analyzing the collected data, educators can gain a deeper understanding of the student's growth trajectory, celebrate milestones, and strategize for challenges.

Step 4: Prepare for IEP Review

Maintaining the relevance and adaptability of a student's IEP requires diligent preparation for periodic reviews. Leaders can strengthen this critical phase by implementing the following strategies.

- **Emphasize the importance of meticulous documentation:** Encourage educators to maintain a detailed record of the student's progress, challenges, and any interventions implemented. This creates a robust foundation for insightful discussions during the review.

- **Advocate for a team-centric approach:** Consider facilitating collaborative spaces where all stakeholders, from educators to therapists and family members, can share resources. This collective input enriches the review process and guarantees a comprehensive understanding of the student's current situation.

- **Offer training related to data interpretation:** Equip educators with skills to analyze and present the data collected to ensure that the review discussions are grounded in concrete evidence and clear insights.

- **Initiate mock review sessions, if necessary:** These can serve as a preparatory platform, enabling educators to refine their presentation skills, anticipate potential questions, and align on key talking points.

- **Provide resources to streamline review preparation:** Resources like templates and guidelines can help educators structure their findings and recommendations effectively. See the Takeaway Tool Kit (page 111) offered at the end of this chapter.

- **Encourage open communication:** Ensure that any concerns, suggestions, or updates from the broader team are communicated promptly, allowing for timely adjustments and informed discussions during the review.

- **Highlight the importance of feedback post-review:** Collecting insights on the review process itself can shed light on areas for improvement, ensuring that subsequent reviews are even more effective and impactful.

In the complex journey of the IEP process, each step, stakeholder, and strategy are pivotal waypoints. When navigated with diligence and understanding, these waypoints connect to form a route that's tailored to meet the unique needs of each student. I've witnessed efficient and effective pre- and post-IEP practices, and I've also experienced broken processes where team members did not collaborate outside of annual IEP meetings and did not implement accommodations. Not only does this often adversely impact our learners, but it can also overburden our case managers.

By actively guiding these processes, you can reinforce a culture of collaboration where every stakeholder feels supported and valued. It is essential that leaders foster an environment where resources are readily accessible and systems of support are effective. Creating a supportive environment with easy-to-access resources is a game changer. And here's the real win: When leaders effectively supervise and support the pre- and post-IEP co-planning, it can positively contribute to special educators' perception of administrative support. Truly, it should be a team effort dedicated to putting students first and keeping everyone in sync.

IEP Meeting Scenarios

With the foundational steps of the pre- and post-IEP process outlined, it's time to see these principles in action. The concept of collaborative IEP processes comes to life more vividly when applied in real-world contexts, where challenges and opportunities uniquely shape their implementation.

The approaches to these critical steps can vary widely depending on the uniqueness of the school context. Whether in a traditional brick-and-mortar school or an innovative online learning environment, the principles of collaboration, co-planning, and adaptability remain at the heart of the process.

The following scenarios highlight how two schools—Golden Light Elementary and Horizon E-Academy—implement the pre- and post-IEP processes. These examples illustrate how tailored approaches, unique to each school's context, can bring the guiding principles of effective IEP creation and implementation to life.

In-Person Pre-IEP Meeting Scenario: Golden Light Elementary

At Golden Light Elementary, the preparatory IEP process is a collective endeavor, kicking off weeks before the actual meeting. The principal sets the tone by equipping the team with practical tools like the electronic

"Pre-IEP Group Feedback Form" (figure 4.2, page 114). This form helps teachers and staff meticulously gather details about a student's progress, challenges, and strengths. The process feels like assembling a jigsaw puzzle, where each piece of information contributes to a complete and meaningful picture of the student.

Take, for example, Ms. Parker, the speech specialist. She has a natural ability to connect with students, making her interactions both engaging and revealing. During a casual yet intentional conversation with one student, she uncovered the child's passion for graphic novels—a detail that became a creative entry point for fostering engagement and learning. This moment of discovery not only informed her strategies but also underscored the importance of seeing the whole student.

Then there's Mr. Lee, the case manager, whose talent for building rapport with families is a cornerstone of the school's approach. Supported by the leadership's commitment to open communication, Mr. Lee regularly schedules teleconferences with parents or guardians. One such call evolved into a heartfelt discussion where a parent shared aspirations and goals for their child that the team hadn't previously considered. This input enriched the IEP, making it reflect both the student's needs and the family's vision for success.

When the staff gather for their ideation session, it's far from a perfunctory meeting. Guided by the principal's emphasis on collaboration, these sessions become dynamic workshops where teachers and specialists exchange ideas, refine strategies, and craft a cohesive plan for the IEP meeting. It's not just about checking boxes—it's about creating a framework that sets the stage for meaningful discussions and actionable outcomes.

Virtual School Pre-IEP Meeting Scenario: Horizon E-Academy

Horizon E-Academy has really embraced the digital space to make sure every student is supported, no matter the miles between them. The preparatory IEP process here has the same heart as Golden Light's, but it's all done with a tech-savvy twist.

Educators get together on their virtual playground—a communal web portal—where they can pop in student data, share insights, and bounce ideas off each other. Think of it as a digital bulletin board where sticky notes from teachers all over the map come together.

Mrs. Hamilton, the counselor with a gentle knack for virtual chats, sets up video calls that feel as close to a cozy office sit-down as you can get online. She has a gift for making screens and miles disappear, helping students open up about their school life.

Then there's Mr. Rodriguez, who has mastered a seamless email-to-digital-dialogue dance. He starts with emails to guardians that are so inviting that they naturally lead to deeper, meaningful exchanges in a digital discussion space. It's almost as if they're gathering around a virtual kitchen table, sharing stories and their dreams for their kids.

By the time everything lands on their group platform, it feels like they've stitched together a quilt of experiences, ready to wrap around the upcoming online IEP meeting. It's this blend of technology and personal touch that sets the stage for a discussion that's as connected as any in-person gathering.

In-Person Post-IEP Meeting Scenario: Golden Light Elementary

After an IEP meeting at Golden Light Elementary, collaborative action kicks into gear. Following the meeting, the special education team convenes a thorough post-meeting staff session. Here, they dive deep into the IEP specifics, ensuring unanimous understanding and commitment. They emphasize forging a co-planning practice between general and special education teachers. For instance, Mrs. O'Neal, the special education teacher, regularly supports Mr. Martin, a general educator, on tailoring accommodations for specific tests or class assignments. Their synergy exemplifies the spirit of collaborative support, which is vital for effective IEP implementation. Mr. Davis, the special education coordinator, initiates a system for routine check-ins, continually assessing the effectiveness and nuances of the accommodations and goals. Parents remain closely involved, receiving timely updates about their child's milestones.

Virtual School Post-IEP Meeting Scenario: Horizon E-Academy

Upon the IEP meeting's conclusion at Horizon E-Academy, the digital collaborative space is promptly updated. In this virtual realm, co-planning practices are championed. Mr. Peters, a special education expert, works collaboratively with Mr. Thompson, the general education instructor, guiding him on integrating specific accommodations into online assignments and evaluations. Their digital interactions foster an environment of shared responsibility and expertise. Regular virtual check-ins are earmarked, led by Mr. Thompson and Mr. Peters, to reflect on the IEP's progression and recalibrate based on real-time insights. Mrs. Adams, the online school therapist, supplements her expertise with resources and advice, especially in navigating online-specific challenges. Parents are kept in the loop through electronic reports and periodic virtual discussions to ensure they are active participants in their child's academic journey.

In the virtual setting of Horizon E-Academy, the collaborative dynamics highlight a proactive approach to special education where continuous communication and adaptation play critical roles. As this scenario unfolds, it underscores the importance of agility and thoroughness in addressing the unique needs of each student.

Whether at Golden Light Elementary or Horizon E-Academy, these scenarios demonstrate the transformative power of collaboration in the IEP process. From assembling insights during the pre-meeting phase to fostering ongoing communication and adaptation post-meeting, both schools highlight the importance of tailoring strategies to their unique contexts. While Golden Light emphasizes the interpersonal connections fostered through in-person engagement, Horizon E-Academy showcases the innovative use of digital tools to bridge distances and create meaningful interactions. Don't be mistaken, though—technology isn't just for virtual schools; it can also revolutionize in-person practices, making processes more efficient and accessible for all team members. Together, these examples show that regardless of the setting, the heart of effective IEP implementation lies in a commitment to teamwork, creativity, and adaptability.

Tips From the Top

As a school leader, you know that collaboration is the backbone of much of what we do in education, especially in relation to IEPs, which mandate collective commitment. Still, it's not without hurdles. Misalignments in team perspectives or the complexity of scheduling can slow things down. To pave the way for smoother collaboration, establish a culture of open communication where every team member feels valued and heard. Consider setting up regular, structured meetings with clear agendas. These should be more than just check-ins—they're opportunities to actively engage with and integrate diverse perspectives.

Embrace technology to streamline communication. Platforms like Google Workspace (https://workspace.google.com) or Microsoft Teams (www.microsoft.com/en-us/microsoft-teams) can be game changers, fostering space for team members to share updates, access documents in real time, and maintain continuous dialogue. These tools aren't just administrative conveniences—they are vital in ensuring everyone stays on the same page, no matter their location or time zone.

As a leader, you are the anchor in the IEP process, providing direction, clarity, and support to ensure the team operates cohesively and with purpose. Encourage your team to explore creative solutions to challenges and ensure they feel supported in their roles. By fostering a supportive environment, you're not just managing a process—you're leading a team that makes real differences in students' lives.

Voices From the Field

The following vignette is shared by Sharon, an experienced Learning Disabilities Teacher-Consultant in New Jersey. With over thirty years of experience working in diverse school settings, Sharon brings a wealth of knowledge to planning and facilitating effective IEP meetings. Her approach focuses on creating compassionate, inclusive environments where all stakeholders—students, families, teachers, and specialists—feel heard and valued. Sharon's story affirms the importance of collaboration, clear communication, and a commitment to student-centered practices, aligning seamlessly with this chapter's focus on preparing and implementing collaborative IEPs.

NURTURING IEP MEETINGS

Planning and facilitating effective eligibility and IEP meetings where students, parents, guardians, teachers, administrators, service providers, and evaluators can all comfortably contribute is challenging. In New Jersey, the Department of Education's approach to special education includes the pivotal Child Study Team, comprising a school social worker, a school psychologist, and a Learning Disabilities Teacher–Consultant. This unique position ensures that someone with teaching experience and expertise in academic achievement is part of the evaluation and planning processes for students who are eligible for special education services.

After my first year as a kindergarten teacher, I was desperate to understand more about how children learn and how to reach and teach them more effectively, so I enrolled in graduate courses that summer to become a Learning Disabilities Teacher–Consultant. Over the next thirty years, I worked in various school settings with diverse student populations. Through this experience, I realized the importance of creating a safe space in IEP and special education meetings for all stakeholders to share their expertise and thoughts. This realization led to the creation of Nurturing IEP Meetings, an extension of my Nurturing Student Success program.

There are several components to our IEP meeting process. They are student-centered and prioritize the voices of the student and their family to ensure their perspectives are heard and valued. The meetings are teacher friendly; consultations are provided before meetings to ensure teachers are prepared and comfortable, enabling them to focus on teaching. Utilizing compassionate communication, the Nurtured Heart Approach®, and trauma-informed practices creates a supportive environment. Clearly defining roles, responsibilities, meeting purposes, next steps, language, and terms ensures everyone is on the same page. And finally, our IEP meetings are code based, utilizing federal and state special education regulations as the basis for programs and services to ensure compliance and best practices.

Our approach to IEP meetings has significantly improved their effectiveness. By focusing on creating a compassionate and inclusive environment, we have been able to develop more effective and individualized education plans. Teachers appreciate the support and clarity provided; parents feel their concerns and insights are valued; and students benefit from plans that truly address their unique needs.

—Sharon Davis, Educational Consultant and Diagnostician, New Jersey

Takeaway Tool Kit

Navigating the world of IEPs demands both preparation and reflection. To streamline this process, I provide three starter tools that act as bookends to the IEP journey for your teachers.

Figure 4.2 (page 114) is a pre-IEP tool that supports gathering critical data and capturing a student's academic performance, personal development, classroom engagement, and existing accommodations. Creating this tool was a dream for me! As a former special education teacher and program director, I know firsthand how important tools such as this one can be. Yes, it's simple—but the purpose of it is to provide a foundation for collaboratively collecting and sharing information.

This form can also be converted into an electronic survey form. In fact, immediately following figure 4.2, I provide guidance on how you might further digitally transform this tool. It can be life-changing for the special education team. This tool provides a holistic overview that empowers educators to approach IEP meetings with clarity, for informed and effective decision making.

Before you review this form, I would be remiss if I didn't take this opportunity to provide some descriptions that you, as a school leader, might find insightful. For those of you who don't need this friendly reminder, please skip ahead to the "Pre-IEP Group Feedback Form" (figure 4.2, page 114). The following descriptions might help enhance participants' understanding of the areas in which case managers are seeking feedback and potentially guide them in providing feedback that case managers find most relevant.

- **Social-emotional development:** This refers to a student's ability to understand and manage their emotions, form meaningful relationships, and navigate social interactions. It includes:
  - *Emotional regulation*—Ability to cope with frustration, manage stress, or express emotions appropriately
  - *Social skills*—Engaging in positive interactions with peers and adults, sharing, and participating in group activities
  - *Empathy*—Recognizing and understanding the emotions of others
  - *Self-concept*—Confidence in their abilities, self-esteem, and understanding their role within a group
- **Behavioral development:** This encompasses a student's actions and reactions in various settings as well as their ability to follow rules and meet behavioral expectations. It includes:
  - *Self-control*—Impulse management, ability to stay on task, and avoiding disruptive behaviors
  - *Compliance*—Following directions from adults, adhering to classroom norms, and completing assignments

- *Behavioral challenges*—Any patterns of aggression, defiance, withdrawal, or other behaviors impacting learning
- *Adaptability*—Flexibility in adjusting to changes in routine or environment

- **Communication development:** This area addresses a student's ability to effectively express themselves and understand others, covering both verbal and nonverbal skills. It includes:
  - *Expressive language*—Using words, phrases, or other methods to convey thoughts, needs, and feelings
  - *Receptive language*—Understanding and interpreting verbal and nonverbal communication from others
  - *Social communication*—Pragmatic language skills such as initiating conversations, taking turns in dialogue, and understanding social cues
  - *Alternative communication*—Use of assistive devices, sign language, or visual supports, if applicable

- **Physical development:** This pertains to the student's physical abilities and how they affect participation in educational activities. It includes:
  - *Gross motor skills*—Abilities involving larger movements, such as walking, running, or climbing
  - *Fine motor skills*—Precise movements like writing, cutting, or manipulating small objects
  - *Sensory needs*—Responses to sensory input, including sensitivities to sound, light, textures, or other environmental stimuli
  - *Health considerations*—Physical conditions or medical needs that may impact the student's participation in school activities, such as mobility aids or fatigue management

Pre-IEP Group Feedback Form

Student's Name: _____ Grade: _____

Due Date: _____

Academic Performance

Subject or Area	Grade Level	Achievements or Strengths	Growth Areas
Mathematics			
Reading			
Writing			
Science			
Social Studies			
Other: _____			

Personal Development

Development Area	Achievements or Strengths	Growth Areas
Social-Emotional		
Behavioral		
Communication		
Physical		
Other: _____		

Classroom Participation and Engagement

Participation: ☐ Always ☐ Often ☐ Sometimes ☐ Rarely ☐ Never

Interactions With Peers: ☐ Excellent ☐ Adequate ☐ Seldom ☐ Needs improvement

Comments on Participation and Engagement:

Accommodations

Intervention or Accommodation	Effectiveness	Comments
	☐ Highly effective ☐ Effective ☐ Somewhat effective ☐ Not effective	
	☐ Highly effective ☐ Effective ☐ Somewhat effective ☐ Not effective	

Additional Notes or Observations

Recommendations for Upcoming IEP

Figure 4.2: Pre-IEP group feedback form.

Visit go.SolutionTree.com/specialneeds for a free reproducible version of this figure.

Here is how you can transform the paper or Word version of the preceding template into an interactive technological tool.

- **Digitize the process:** Moving the form to a digital format such as Google Forms (https://workspace.google.com/products/forms), Microsoft Forms (https://forms.office.com), or a dedicated platform allows for easier data entry, real-time collaboration, and automated aggregation of responses. You can do this by:
    - Including drop-downs or checkboxes for frequently used fields
    - Using conditional logic to tailor sections based on responses (for example, having a field appear for specific feedback for areas checked as "needs improvement")
    - Generating a summary report automatically from the inputs
- **Add inclusive elements:** Ensuring accessibility for all educators (including those unfamiliar with certain terminology) increases usability. You can do this by:

- Providing tooltips or examples for fields (for example, on what qualifies as social-emotional challenges or physical development areas)
- Using universal design principles to ensure the form is accessible for staff with disabilities (for example, screen-reader compatibility)

• **Expand qualitative insights:** Qualitative data often provide the most insight into student needs and accommodations. You can do this by:
- Including prompts or guiding questions in the Comments sections (for example, a prompt to describe a specific instance where the accommodation was highly effective)
- Allowing users to upload attachments (for example, student work samples or observation notes)

• **Enhance checkbox sections:** This allows greater specificity. You can do this by incorporating elements such as:
- Participation frequency [Drop-down: Always / Often / Sometimes / Rarely / Never]
- Peer interactions quality [Drop-down: Excellent / Adequate / Seldom / Needs improvement]
- Additional comments on engagement [Option for free text or uploads]

• **Centralize data collection for review:** Centralizing and visualizing data across multiple students saves time and identifies trends. You can do this by:
- Linking the form responses to a dashboard such as Airtable (www.airtable.com) or iTrack (https://itracktwc.com) for easy access and real-time updates
- Allowing for exportable reports that can be shared with the IEP team

Figure 4.3, the "Family Input Form," can enhance case managers' IEP preparation process. This form is designed to capture the invaluable perspectives and insights of families on their child's academic and social-emotional strengths, areas of improvement, current accommodations, and

Family Input Form for IEP Meeting Preparation

Student Information

Student's Name: _____

Date of Birth: _____ School: _____

Case Manager: _____

Introduction

Dear _____,

Your insights and feedback are invaluable to us as we strive to provide the best educational experience for your child. This form is designed to gather your input on your child's academic and social-emotional development as part of the Individualized Education Program (IEP) process. Your responses will help us continue to partner with you in tailoring the educational strategies and supports to better meet your child's unique needs.

If you would prefer to discuss your input in a meeting (by phone, videoconference, or in person), please let me know.

Your Child's Strengths and Areas for Improvement

- Academic strengths: What do you consider to be your child's main academic strengths?

- Social-emotional strengths: What are your child's key strengths in social and emotional development?

- Other strengths: What are your child's strengths in other areas?

- Areas for Improvement: What areas do you think your child needs more support with?

Effectiveness of Current Accommodations or Modifications

- Current accommodations or modifications: What accommodations or modifications is your child currently receiving? Please list them and comment on your perception of their effectiveness.

- Suggestions for changes: Are there accommodations or modifications you feel should be added or adjusted? Please specify.

continued >

Figure 4.3: Family input form.

Progress and Goals
- Progress on current IEP goals: How do you feel about the progress your child is making on their current IEP goals?

- Suggestions for new goals: Are there new areas or goals you believe should be considered in the upcoming IEP? Please describe them.

Additional Supports and Services
- Needed services: Are there specific services or supports (such as speech therapy, occupational therapy, counseling, and so on) that you believe should be included or modified in your child's IEP?

- Service environment: In what school environment do you believe your child should receive the above services (such as general education classes or special education classes)?

General Feedback and Concerns
- Additional comments: Please share any other comments or questions you have that could help us better support your child's learning and development.

Consent to Discuss
- Permission: Do you give consent for the case manager and relevant school personnel to discuss the contents of this form during the IEP meeting?
  ☐ Yes   ☐ No

Please return this form to your child's case manager by _____.
We appreciate your cooperation and value your input.
Thank you for your time and for contributing to your child's educational planning.

*Visit **go.SolutionTree.com/special needs** for a free reproducible version of this figure.*

future goals. By integrating this family feedback, case managers and educators can implement a more person-centered approach in the IEP meetings, fostering greater collaboration and understanding.

Figure 4.4, designed to meticulously monitor IEP goal progress, will come in handy to track and reflect on the set goals and will aid in legal compliance. It provides educators with a consistent structure to assess, refine, and adjust interventions, making sure that the student remains at the heart of the process. Collectively, these tools pave the way for a comprehensive and

Student Information

Name: _____ Grade: _____ Date of Birth: _____
Teacher or Teachers: _____
Start Date of IEP: _____ End Date of IEP: _____

Goal Overview: Use this section to record a concise summary of the student's IEP goals, including measurable objectives and target dates.

Goal Identifier	Description of the Goal	Target Date	Benchmark (if any)

Progress Monitoring

Fill in this table at whatever frequency works best—but at least monthly—based on the individuality of the student and their IEP goals.

Date	Goal Identifier	Method or Tool Used	Data or Results (monthly)

Goal Progress Summary			
Date	Goal Identifier	Progress Status	Comments
		☐ On track ☐ Needs attention ☐ Mastered	
		☐ On track ☐ Needs attention ☐ Mastered	

Supporting Documents and Resources
[Description example: Attachment 1, mathematics assessment from 9/5/24]

Teacher Notes and Reflection
Date:

Next Steps and Recommendations
[Suggested intervention, accommodations, or support strategy based on data noted above]
[Recommendations for changes or continued use of one or more strategies]

Figure 4.4: IEP goal progress monitoring form.

*Visit **go.SolutionTree.com/special needs** for a free reproducible version of this figure.*

effective IEP experience, ensuring both preparedness and purposeful reflection. You can adapt any of these tools to meet the unique needs of your school context. Adapting figure 4.4 (page 119) into a spreadsheet format offers several advantages for tracking and managing IEP goals, especially for educators handling multiple students. A digital spreadsheet enables you to centralize data, automate calculations, and create visuals for easy analysis. Here's how you might implement this.

- **Use tabs for organization.**
    - Create separate tabs for each student or IEP goal category (for example, academic goals, behavioral goals, and so on).
    - Include a master tab for a high-level overview of all goals and their statuses.
- **Automate progress tracking.**
    - Use formulas to calculate percentages or highlight overdue tasks (for example, using conditional formatting to flag benchmarks that are past their target date).
    - Auto-generate progress summaries based on data entered (for example, flagging the goal for review if data show "needs attention" more than twice).
- **Visualize data.**
    - Integrate charts or graphs to represent progress over time, providing a quick reference for teachers, administrators, and families.
- **Facilitate collaboration.**
    - Use platforms like Google Sheets (https://workspace.google.com/products/sheets) or iTrack (https://itracktwc.com) to enable real-time collaboration among educators, allowing multiple team members to update and view progress simultaneously.
- **Create templates.**
    - Build reusable templates with locked headers and drop-downs for fields like "progress status" or "method used," ensuring uniformity across IEP plans.

 **Wrap-Up**

In this chapter, we explored the interconnected steps that make collaborative IEPs a cornerstone of effective special education. By equipping teams with strategies, support, and a shared commitment to student success, you can lead the IEP preparation and follow-through process to be dynamic, inclusive, and impactful.

Transitioning forward, we'll turn our focus to the transformative potential of technology in education. The next chapter will highlight how digital literacy and innovative tools can support educators, enhance professional development, and improve outcomes for students in both physical and virtual classrooms.

Chapter Five

Leveraging Digital Tools, Assistive Technology, and AI

The integration of technology into our school culture and practices is no longer optional—it is an essential component of equity-driven education. As educators, we must continuously strive to provide all students with equitable access to high-quality education. Digital literacy stands at the heart of this mission, serving as a gateway to transforming programs, enhancing work habits, and creating a more efficient, engaging, and supportive environment for school personnel, students, and families.

Consider the rapid growth of online schools, which have become integral to K–12 education. Recent data from the Digital Learning Collaborative (n.d., 2024) indicate that approximately 4.3 million students were enrolled in full-time online schools as of 2024, highlighting the shift toward flexible and accessible learning models in the post-pandemic era (Digital Learning Collaborative, n.d., 2024). Reports like *Snapshot 2024: The Post-Pandemic Digital Learning Landscape Emerges* and profiles from the Proof Points Project showcase how innovations in digital learning are reshaping classrooms—whether virtual, hybrid, or in person—and spotlight the importance of integrating technology effectively into all educational settings (Digital Learning Collaborative, 2024).

As school leaders, your role in championing digital innovations is vital, particularly in addressing the unique challenges faced in special education. By embracing technology and fostering digital literacy, we can equip teachers and students alike with the tools to thrive in an increasingly interconnected educational landscape.

The daily reality for many special education teachers involves high levels of stress and burnout, contributed to by factors like cumbersome paperwork and a lack of effective communication channels and support. The burnout rate among special education teachers is alarmingly high and driven by chronic stress and job dissatisfaction (Robinson et al., 2019). We go more in depth into this topic when we transition to our chapter on workload optimization. Digital technology can be leveraged to alleviate these challenges and support retention of quality educators.

While higher pay is cited as a top recruitment and retention strategy—which is justified given the higher workload of special educators—it is not the only existing strategy, and it should be coupled with immediate and long-term solutions. Professional learning, which we addressed comprehensively in chapter 2 (page 37), and workload management, which we address more in chapter 6 (page 155), are essential and immediate teacher retention strategies that school leaders can implement. The digital technologies I address in this chapter should be considered in support of targeting teacher workloads, professional work habits, and student learning.

Consider the daily challenges educators face in keeping families informed, managing student behavior, and providing personalized feedback. Digital tools offer innovative solutions to these challenges, with each bringing unique features that cater specifically to the needs of special education. These communication tools can support fostering stronger connections among teachers, students, and parents and enhance the overall educational experience.

In this chapter, we will address several digital technologies that can be leveraged to support effective communication among stakeholders, aid in storing and sharing information, and support instructional planning, caseload management, and the facilitation of an accessible learning environment. This chapter is intended to enhance your awareness, or literacy, of digital technologies and their integration, which you can leverage to empower special education, and offers tools to guide and aid your efforts.

Technologies for Effective Communication

Now that we've established the critical importance of effective communication and collaboration throughout this book, let's discuss digital tools that aim to enhance communication between administrators, teachers, students, and families. I'd like to introduce you to these tools in the hope that you'll be inspired to look further into the potential benefits of integrating these or other tools to support communication practices. We'll consider how you can leverage these digital technologies to keep everyone informed and engaged.

There are several technological tools and ways to integrate them. The effectiveness of leveraging digital tools depends on how well they are implemented and integrated into pedagogical routines. When focusing on tools that can serve as conduits to effective communication, consider the importance of accessibility.

Before selecting tools, it's crucial to assess the technological literacy of your teachers, families, and high-school-age students. If you are unsure about their familiarity with technology, find out! Conduct surveys, hold informal discussions, or observe current technology use to gauge their comfort levels. This will help you tailor your approach to integration. For stakeholders with lower tech literacy, consider offering introductory workshops or creating simple, step-by-step guides to help them become comfortable with the chosen tools. For more tech-savvy audiences, focus on advanced features and customization options that maximize the tools' potential. By aligning your implementation strategy with your stakeholders' varying levels of familiarity and confidence with technology, you can create a more inclusive and effective communication system.

Always prioritize student privacy. Make sure your communication tools comply with privacy laws like the Family Educational Rights and Privacy Act (1974). Educate both staff and parents on how to keep information secure online. By maintaining these practices, you can build trust and safeguard the well-being of your students, creating a safe and effective learning environment. By integrating these best practices, school leaders can support special education programs more effectively, aiming to ensure that all students receive the personalized support they need to succeed. This approach not only enhances educational outcomes but also helps retain dedicated teachers by fostering a collaborative and secure environment.

If you are reading this book and you've already considered, or have implemented, digital tools as I discuss them in this chapter, please keep reading and consider how you might reflect on and improve your current practices. While I am not highlighting an exhaustive list of technological tools,

I will talk in detail about several. I will describe the tool, highlight its purpose in special education, and provide integration action steps. As you explore these tools, consider how they might fit into your specific context and needs, and remember that the landscape of educational technology is rich with possibilities and ever-evolving.

Instant Notifications

Keeping families informed can be simple and effective with technology that enables instant notifications and real-time updates. This immediacy is especially critical in special education settings, where timely communication can directly impact student success. Platforms that allow for instant messaging, announcements, behavior tracking, and multimedia sharing provide invaluable tools for fostering stronger connections among parents, students, and teachers.

For example, messaging and announcement tools can allow teachers to share updates about assignments, events, or urgent matters directly with families. Features like behavior tracking, real-time photo or video sharing, and reminders help parents stay connected to their child's educational journey, even daily. Such platforms also support two-way communication by ensuring families can ask questions or share concerns with teachers, enhancing collaboration and trust.

When implementing tools to enhance communication, focus on the functionalities that best meet the needs of your school community. Consider selecting a platform that enables instant messaging for homework reminders, event notifications, or other updates. Look for options that provide multimedia capabilities—such as the ability to share videos, photos, or documents—to keep families engaged and informed about classroom activities and student progress. Additionally, prioritize tools that are user friendly and accessible to families with varying levels of technological literacy.

By adopting a platform with these features, you can create a more inclusive and supportive environment, ensuring that families feel informed, connected, and actively involved in their child's education.

ClassDojo (www.classdojo.com) and Remind (www.remind.com) are two platforms that can be powerful tools for increasing communication with families, and there are several others to consider.

The following are actionable insights for your team to consider.

- **Use of instant messaging:** Determine the specific needs and goals for using instant notifications in your special education context. Identify the key areas where timely communication is crucial and outline how your technology platform can address these needs.

- **Training sessions for teachers:** Provide professional learning sessions for teachers on how to use your platform's features effectively for communication and behavior tracking. Ensure teachers are comfortable with sending messages, setting up reminders, and managing features like class groups.

- **Platform instruction for caregivers:** Educate caregivers on how to use the platform to stay informed about their child's progress and participate in their learning journey. Show them how to receive notifications, respond to messages, and stay engaged with their child's education.

- **Routine for consistent communication:** Encourage teachers to regularly post updates, photos, and videos to keep parents informed about classroom activities, schedules, assignments, and student behavior. Establish a routine for sending out updates to maintain consistent communication.

- **Routine for collecting feedback:** Institute a routine for families and students to provide feedback through the platform to foster an ongoing dialogue and continuous improvement in communication. Use their feedback to refine your communication strategies and ensure that the platform effectively meets the community's needs.

Asynchronous Video

Asynchronous video refers to prerecorded video content that viewers can access at their convenience so participants aren't required to be online at the same time. This flexibility makes it an especially beneficial tool in special education, where visual and auditory aids can significantly enhance understanding and engagement. For instance, teachers can create video tutorials or lesson summaries that allow students to revisit content as needed, catering to diverse learning needs and pacing requirements. Tools such as Loom (www.loom.com) can streamline communication and provide accessible, detailed instruction, making them valuable for enhancing special education programs across various learning environments.

As a school leader, you also can consider how you might leverage video tools when communicating with families and your staff! There are several versatile video messaging tools designed to simplify communication through instantly shareable videos. They permit users to record their screen, camera, and microphone simultaneously, or record using just one option, making them excellent resources for creating detailed instructional content and personalized feedback. As a school leader, consider how tools like these can also enhance communication within your teams and with families and promote a collaborative and inclusive school culture.

Improve engagement and communication in special education by providing a platform for creating and sharing video messages; delivering clear, detailed instructions and personalized feedback; and fostering an inclusive and collaborative learning environment through interactive video discussions. The following are actionable insights for your team to consider.

- **Instructional videos:** Create personalized instructional videos that cater to the specific learning needs of students to ensure they receive tailored support.

- **Visual and auditory features:** Incorporate visual and auditory elements in videos to enhance comprehension and retention for students with diverse learning preferences.

- **Regular updates:** Send regular video updates and instructions to caregivers to help them stay informed about the student's progress and reinforce learning at home. Encourage parents to participate in the learning process by sharing video updates and allowing them to respond with their own videos, enhancing the school-home connection.

- **Personalized guidance and peer interaction:** Record and share personalized video feedback for students, providing clear, detailed guidance they can revisit as needed to improve their work and understanding. Promote peer-to-peer interaction by assigning group projects where students can discuss and collaborate through video responses, building social and communication skills.

- **Training on platform use:** Train special education teachers on how to effectively use your platform to create engaging and informative content, enhance their teaching strategies, and foster a more interactive and supportive learning environment.

Now that we've discussed some of the dynamic features and benefits of communication tools, it's essential to consider how to maximize their effectiveness. Thoughtful implementation of these technologies can significantly enhance communication between staff, educators, students, and parents, fostering a more efficient, inclusive, and supportive educational environment. Moreover, quick feedback and real-time data sharing can greatly improve teachers' work habits. Immediate access to information allows teachers to make timely adjustments, share insights, and collaborate more effectively, ultimately boosting the overall effectiveness of special education programs.

Digital Class Ecosystem

A digital class ecosystem has the potential to make a positive impact on your team's administrative and case management workloads. Time and stress saved by effectively leveraging technology for things like progress tracking, personalizing assignments, and providing feedback, among other things, may enable teachers to dedicate more time to direct instruction and personalized student support. Tools such as Seesaw (https://web.seesaw.me) can be valuable digital resources that can be leveraged to enhance the efficacy, accessibility, and workload management of special programs. Seesaw is a digital learning platform designed to facilitate communication, collaboration, and engagement between educators, students, and families, aiming to enhance the classroom experience. Tools similar to Seesaw are teacher-driven and often offer an organized space for students to document their learning and receive personalized feedback, making them especially beneficial for hybrid and online schools. Customizable features can be leveraged to support implementation of accommodations and modifications. In my experience, once teachers are trained and effectively supported, they find it easy to tailor assignments and resources to facilitate individualized support.

Google Classroom (https://classroom.google.com) is another platform that can be an effective tool for supporting special education programs across various learning environments, including in person, hybrid, and online. Its user-friendly and flexible design helps teachers streamline communication, organize coursework, and offer personalized support to students with diverse needs. The intuitive interface simplifies assignment management, making it accessible for both educators and students. Teachers can easily customize assignments to provide necessary accommodations and modifications.

Integrated tools like Google Meet (https://meet.google.com) and Google Hangouts (https://hangouts.google.com) facilitate real-time communication, enhancing engagement among teachers, students, and parents. Additionally, features such as shared documents and instant feedback foster a collaborative learning environment. Google Classroom's integration with assistive technologies can help ensure that all students can access and effectively engage with learning materials. Digital ecosystems like Seesaw and Google Classroom not only simplify administrative tasks but also empower teachers to focus on personalized instruction and support, making them invaluable for special education.

Enhance the efficacy, accessibility, and workload management of special education programs by integrating a teacher-driven digital class ecosystem platform, of your team's choice, that supports individualized learning, fosters continuous engagement, and integrates seamlessly with various learning environments and assistive technologies. The following are actionable insights for your team to consider.

- **Specialized professional learning opportunities:** A recurring theme of this book! Conduct comprehensive, targeted training experiences for special education teachers and anyone who supports students with IEPs, focusing on how to leverage your digital ecosystem's features to accommodate diverse learning needs. Provide continuous opportunities, such as webinars and workshops, to keep educators updated on best practices and new features. Be sure to consider your teachers' needs and desires when planning professional development.

- **Dedicated support system:** Create a collaborative support network where teachers can share resources, best practices, and solutions to common challenges related to using your digital ecosystem. Establish a dedicated help desk or support team to assist teachers with technical issues and provide troubleshooting assistance for platform-related problems.

- **Customized implementation:** Use customizable features that teachers can utilize to create and distribute assignments tailored to each student's unique needs to ensure appropriate accommodations and modifications are in place. Develop universally designed learning materials and resources that cater to various learning styles and levels to maximize student engagement and understanding.

- **Enhanced family engagement:** Use robust, user-friendly communication tools to keep families informed and involved in their child's learning journey, providing regular updates and feedback about their child's progress, upcoming assignments, and any changes in their education plan. Offer training and support sessions for families to help them navigate the ecosystem and stay engaged with their child's progress and school activities. Ensure all communication is accessible to all caregivers, including those who may not be tech-savvy, by providing guides and tutorials.

- **Efficient progress monitoring:** Support teachers in implementing progress-tracking features to monitor student performance and make timely adjustments to instruction as needed. Make use of the collected data to inform instructional strategies and interventions, aiming to ensure that each student receives the necessary support to succeed.

- **Inclusive learning environment:** Integrate your ecosystem with various assistive technologies (such as screen readers or speech-to-text tools) to enhance accessibility for students often disabled by our systems. Customize the platform to include features that enhance accessibility, such as captions for videos, alternative text for images, and easy-to-navigate course materials.

- **Regular evaluation and feedback:** Don't miss this insight! Continuously evaluate the impact of your digital ecosystem on student engagement, learning outcomes, and teacher workload to identify areas for improvement. Use surveys, feedback forms, and analytics to gather data. Establish a feedback loop with teachers, students, and families to gather insights and refine the use of your ecosystem to ensure it meets the evolving needs of the educational community. Based on evaluation results, continuously refine and adjust use to better meet the needs of your students and improve teaching practices.

Effective Technology Integration in Special Education

Now that we've explored some technological tools, let's consider the essential conditions for successfully integrating those tools into your practices and programs. Effective technology use is about selecting the right tools and implementing them in a way that truly enhances learning and teaching.

Jeffrey P. Bakken and Festus E. Obiakor (2023), in their work *Using Technology to Enhance Special Education*, emphasize that technology integration must go beyond simply providing tools—it must focus on enhancing instructional practices and supporting the individualized needs of students with disabilities. Their research points to case studies where the thoughtful use of assistive technology significantly improved student engagement and academic outcomes, underlining the importance of professional development and planning for successful implementation. One resource that can help you navigate this integration is Jennifer Gonzalez's (2024) *Teacher's Guide to Tech 2024*. This comprehensive handbook simplifies how to learn technology by grouping over 750 technological tools into over fifty categories, and it's updated annually. It explains each tool in clear, simple language and provides practical ideas for using them both in and out of the classroom.

The insights of Bakken and Obiakor (2023) encourage the importance of planning, equity, and ongoing professional growth in leveraging technology effectively. Whether in a traditional classroom or an online setting, technological pedagogy has the potential to transform how we teach and learn when it's implemented with care and intention.

Technologies to Support Documentation Storage and Project Management

The administrative burdens teachers and support staff report are significant. The extensive paperwork, coordination of interventions, and communication requirements often lead to high levels of stress and burnout (Robinson et al., 2019). Research by Olivia Robinson, Shannon Bridges, Lauren Rollins and Randall E. Schumacker (2019) highlights that managing extensive documentation is a major source of stress for special education teachers, contributing to high attrition rates in the field. Manageable workloads and adequate resources are essential for job satisfaction (Ansley, Houchins, & Varjas, 2019). To address these challenges, it is crucial to leverage digital solutions for efficient documentation and secure storage of educational records and student data (Courduff, Szapkiw, & Wendt, 2016; Sheninger, 2019).

Efficient documentation and data management systems not only alleviate administrative burdens but also enhance operational efficiency and student learning outcomes. By integrating these technologies, school leaders can ensure compliance with legal standards and improve accessibility for all stakeholders.

Efficiently collecting and storing information and using data management tools are persistent challenges educators and support staff face. Traditionally, teachers print and complete forms for multiple students, then scan and email these documents to the special education coordinator—a process that is both time-consuming and prone to errors. In online schools, staff complete forms electronically and email them to the special education case manager.

There are technological tools that can assist in facilitating better organization and documentation practices as a means of effective pedagogy (Courduff et al., 2016). iTrack (https://itracktwc.com), mentioned in chapter 4 (page 93), is one platform that offers a solution to these problems by providing a centralized location that streamlines the IEP or 504 process, saving educators significant time and reducing administrative burdens (Business Observer, 2023). Built for nonprofits and elementary, middle, and high schools working with underserved youth at risk, iTrack is a collaborative platform that houses student information and progress so that they can be meticulously tracked and efficiently managed. As school leaders, you may find this tool, and others like it, invaluable for four reasons: (1) It aims to centralize the management of IEP and 504 plans, making it easier for educators to update and share information; (2) it provides actionable insights that help educators make informed decisions about student interventions and supports; (3) its digitized data collection and management eliminate the need for manual form completion and scanning; and (4) it can be customized to fit the needs of any educational setting.

Robust project management platforms offer versatile and visual systems for managing tasks, tracking progress, and facilitating collaboration. Todd Cherner and Douglas Smith (2017) expand on this by discussing how technology tools can facilitate collaborative planning among special education and general education teachers, enhancing integrated teaching approaches. This collaboration is crucial for creating cohesive instructional strategies that benefit all students. By using collaborative platforms and tools, educators can share resources, plan lessons together, and ensure that UDL principles are effectively incorporated into both synchronous and asynchronous learning environments.

In the following sections, I will discuss how project management tools can be leveraged to support special education. I'll also provide actionable steps that you, as a school leader, can implement to empower your teachers and ultimately improve the educational experience for your students.

Project Management

Project management tools can help us create a more streamlined, collaborative, and supportive environment that addresses the unique challenges of special education, promotes teacher retention, and fosters student success.

For instance, Monday (https://monday.com) delivers an adoptable solution for organizing projects and managing workflows. Special education teachers and partner educators can leverage platforms like Monday to organize their schedules, track student progress, and manage IEP goals. Its visual layout helps educators keep track of multiple tasks and deadlines, significantly reducing the administrative burden.

Asana (www.asana.com) acts as an all-encompassing task management platform where educators can devise detailed project plans, allocate tasks, and establish deadlines. These capabilities are particularly useful for special education teams that need to coordinate efforts across various interventions and support plans. Asana connects effortlessly with other tools, putting all the vital information you need at your immediate disposal and streamlining your workflow.

Trello (https://trello.com) uses boards, lists, and cards to create visual task management systems. Special educators and partner educators can use tools like Trello to break down large projects into manageable tasks, track progress, and collaborate with colleagues. Trello's flexibility means your team can tailor it to tasks like planning instruction and tracking activities and deadlines.

Streamline project management and enhance collaboration among special education teams by providing flexible and visual task management platforms. While the many technological tools I mention in this chapter may not be around for the lifetime of this book, I would be remiss to write this chapter without mentioning any tools. My aim is to make connections with present-day technological tools. The following are actionable insights for you to consider for enhancing project and workload management.

- **Task scheduling:** Establish schedules that outline daily, weekly, and monthly tasks for special education teachers and include specific IEP goals, deadlines, and reminders. Be sure to regularly review and adjust schedules and IEP tracking to ensure they align with educational objectives and student needs, and do this in partnership with your special education team. I cannot recommend this enough.
- **Project plans:** Develop comprehensive project plans that include detailed task assignments, deadlines, and milestones, and facilitate collaboration among special education teams by assigning tasks and sharing updates.

- **Task progress-monitoring boards:** Create boards that break down larger work projects into smaller, manageable tasks and track the progress of tasks and projects to ensure timely completion and to identify any areas needing additional support.

Enhanced Virtual Communication and Collaboration

The seamless integration of communication and teamwork is pivotal to any successful special education program. While project management tools like Monday, Asana, and Trello are invaluable for organizing tasks and tracking progress, comprehensive collaboration applications like Microsoft Teams (www.microsoft.com/en-us/microsoft-teams), Zoom (https://zoom.us), and Slack (https://slack.com) offer unique features that elevate real-time communication and seamless document sharing. As a school leader, leveraging Microsoft Teams can significantly enhance the collaborative efforts of special education staff, streamline administrative processes, and improve engagement with parents. The following are practical ways these tools can be utilized to elevate your special education program.

- **Virtual meetings:** Use virtual meetings among special education staff to ensure that everyone can participate regardless of their location. This capability can be crucial for maintaining regular communication, especially in hybrid or remote learning environments. Videoconferencing allows for face-to-face interactions, making meetings more personal and effective.

- **Document sharing:** Share important documents such as IEPs, progress reports, and lesson plans within your collaboration platform. This centralization of information ensures that all relevant documents are easily accessible to staff members, reducing the time spent searching for files and enhancing collaborative planning. With Microsoft Teams, for example, the integration with OneDrive allows for seamless document management and real-time updates.

- **Real-time communication:** Use instant messaging to quickly address any issues or updates. This real-time communication capability improves responsiveness and support, allowing educators to tackle problems as they arise. The chat function also supports threaded conversations, making it easy to follow discussions and decisions.

- **Family engagement:** Provide regular updates to families on student progress and facilitate virtual parent-teacher meetings. Virtual meetings enhance the school-home connection by ensuring families are informed and involved in their child's education. The ease of scheduling and conducting virtual meetings can accommodate caregivers' busy schedules, fostering better relationships and collaboration.

After our discussion on technologies for effective communication, documentation, and project management, I trust you feel both encouraged and empowered. Even if these tools are familiar to you, I hope you now see how you can leverage them to make a substantial impact on efficiency, pedagogy, and student learning. These tools have the potential to transform the lives of your entire educational community—from support staff to families, students, and teachers. They are essential for enhancing special education teacher retention and overall program success. The tools mentioned here are just a few among many. I encourage you to seriously consider which technological tools your team could benefit from.

AI in Special Education

Integrating artificial intelligence (AI) into special education can revolutionize how we support students and staff by personalizing learning experiences, streamlining administrative tasks, enhancing engagement, and enabling efficient, data-driven decision making. As school leaders, you can be a champion of these advancements to improve program outcomes and empower your instructional team. While some may be skeptical of AI, it is essential to develop a deep understanding of its purpose, functionality, and safety measures. Including a discussion on AI in this chapter was not just an option but a necessity given its transformative potential. I am going to share some tips on how AI can be leveraged in special education to support personalized learning, IEP management, administrative efficiency, instructional practices, and data-driven decision making.

Generative AI chatbots like ChatGPT (https://chatgpt.com) are some of the most versatile AI tools available. With their constant evolution, they—and other AI tools—have the potential to address many functions that other specialized tools can't. Educators can leverage generative AI to develop lesson plans, generate ideas for instructional strategies, and provide real-time feedback on educational content. It can also aid in the management of IEPs by suggesting goal modifications based on student progress data, ensuring compliance with legal requirements, and offering recommendations for individualized strategies.

Additionally, generative AI can automate administrative tasks such as scheduling, grading, and communication, thus allowing teachers to focus more on direct instruction and student interaction. By incorporating AI, educators can enhance engagement through interactive dialogue, supporting students' learning and development in a more dynamic and personalized manner. These multifaceted tools exemplify how AI can be used to improve various aspects of special education, making it an invaluable resource for teachers and school leaders alike.

Let's explore additional AI-related benefits and tools that you can utilize to support your goals for empowering special education.

Personalized Learning and IEPs

I conducted a study across nine online schools on credentialed general and special educators' perceptions of their preparedness, knowledge, and practices that leverage technology to support diverse learners in online schools (Wall, 2023, 2024). My findings revealed a dire need for increased training and support for online educators in the effective use of technology to meet the needs of students with disabilities. While many teachers acknowledged the potential of digital tools to individualize instruction, I identified significant gaps in their confidence and preparedness to fully use these resources. This clearly shows the importance of equipping online educators with targeted professional development and support in areas such as adaptive learning technologies, IEP management tools, and digital pedagogy.

Research on online learning highlights the unique opportunities digital platforms provide to personalize instruction for students with disabilities, particularly in virtual and hybrid environments (Rice & Dykeman, 2014). Technology, when implemented strategically, can empower educators to meet the diverse needs of learners, fostering both academic growth and a sense of inclusion (Rice & Dykeman, 2014.) These perspectives align with the broader educational imperative to thoughtfully integrate technology to support and enhance pedagogy.

The following are ways AI can help with adaptive learning and IEP optimization.

- **Adaptive learning technologies:** AI-powered platforms can be leveraged to create personalized learning experiences by adapting content with consideration of each student's needs. These technologies analyze student data to identify strengths and weaknesses, tailoring lessons to individuality and pace (Holmes, Bialik, & Fadel, 2019). For example, tools like DreamBox (www.dreambox.com) and Lexia (www.lexialearning.com) adapt mathematics and reading instruction based on real-time student performance, providing immediate feedback and adjusting the difficulty of tasks.

- **Enhanced IEP management:** AI can be used to streamline the development and management of IEPs. Intelligent systems can track student progress, suggest goal modifications, and ensure compliance with legal requirements (Smith, 2021). Tools like IEP Writer (www.iepwriter.com), MagicSchool (www.magicschool.ai), and Goalbook (https://goalbookapp.com) help teachers create and manage IEPs efficiently by using AI to recommend goals and track student achievements.

The integration of these tools goes beyond technological advancement—these practices aim to transform the educational experience for your school community.

Administrative Efficiency and Teacher Support

The following are ways AI can help improve administration and support practices.

- **Administrative task automation:** AI can be leveraged to reduce the administrative burden on special education teachers by automating repetitive tasks such as grading, scheduling, and data entry. This can support teachers' focus on instruction and student interaction (Li, 2020). Platforms like Gradescope (www.gradescope.com) and Classcraft (www.hmhco.com/programs/classcraft) use AI to automate grading and attendance, freeing up valuable time for teachers.

- **Professional development:** AI-driven professional learning platforms can offer personalized training for teachers, focusing on areas where they need the most improvement. These systems can recommend resources, track progress, and provide feedback (Rodman, 2019).

Student Engagement and Collaboration

The following are ways AI can support student engagement and collaboration.

- **AI-powered communication tools:** AI can be leveraged to facilitate communication between special education teachers, general education teachers, service partners, and parents. Chatbots and virtual assistants can provide instant answers to common questions, schedule meetings, and send reminders (Passow, 2019; Slagg, 2024). Platforms like Remind (www.remind.com) and ClassDojo (www.classdojo.com) incorporate AI to enhance communication and collaboration so you can ensure everyone stays informed and connected.

- **Interactive and engaging learning environments:** AI can be used to create interactive and engaging learning environments using virtual reality and augmented reality. These technologies can support our diverse learners in understanding complex concepts and staying engaged in their learning (Radu, 2014). Tools like Nearpod (https://nearpod.com) and CoSpaces Edu (www.cospaces.io) use AI to create immersive learning experiences that cater to the unique needs of our students.

Data-Driven Decision Making

The following are ways AI can support data-driven decision making.

- **Predictive analytics:** Consider using AI to support analyzing large unidentified sets of data to predict student outcomes, identify at-promise students, and suggest interventions. These capabilities allow educators to make data-driven decisions that enhance student success (Baker & Siemens, 2014). Platforms like BrightBytes (www.brightbytes.net) use predictive analytics to help schools identify trends and make informed decisions about resource allocation and intervention strategies.

- **Monitoring and reporting:** Explore how AI might support the accuracy and efficiency of monitoring and reporting student progress. AI systems can generate detailed reports, track long-term trends, and provide insights into the effectiveness of instructional strategies (Kumar, 2020). AI-powered dashboards in Edmentum (www.edmentum.com) provide real-time data on student performance, which help educators monitor progress and adjust instruction accordingly.

Real-Time Adjustments in Teaching Strategies

AI enables real-time adjustments in teaching strategies based on student responses. How neat! Adaptive learning technologies can monitor student performance in real time and adjust the difficulty level of tasks or provide additional resources as needed (Robinson et al., 2019). Platforms like DreamBox (www.dreambox.com) or Smart Sparrow (www.smartsparrow.com) offer real-time analytics that help teachers understand how students engage with the material, allowing for immediate instructional adjustments.

By carefully considering how your teams can incorporate the use of AI, you can create a more dynamic and responsive learning environment that supports student learning while reducing teachers' stress and workload. Aligning these technological advancements with research findings provides a solid foundation for integrating AI into special education settings, ultimately leading to better educational outcomes and improved teacher retention (Robinson et al., 2019). Be sure to connect with a team of experts when exploring your options and collectively determining the appropriate technological tools to meet the needs of your school community.

Ethical Considerations and Benefits

While AI and other technological advances offer numerous benefits, ethical considerations must be addressed. Privacy and data security are paramount given the sensitive nature of student information in special education. Ensuring transparency in how AI systems make decisions and avoiding biases in AI algorithms are critical to maintaining trust and fairness in educational settings (Holmes et al., 2019; Robinson et al., 2019). I strongly recommend your administrative school team seek further guidance and develop policies and guidelines regarding the use of AI. For example, consider explicitly stating specific student information that is prohibited from being shared. In this case, you'd cite legal mandates in support of this, as well as other relevant school policies regarding confidentiality.

Ethical considerations are integral to leveraging AI and other technologies in education. By prioritizing data privacy, transparency, and fairness, you can build trust and equity in their technological practices. Developing clear policies and adhering to legal mandates ensures that these tools are used responsibly to support students and educators alike.

Tips From the Top

We know the journey of integrating technology isn't always straightforward; tight budgets, the unknown purpose of it all, resistance to change, and the ongoing need for professional development can make it seem daunting. Let me assure you that with proper understanding, support, effective use, and a known need, these challenges can be transformed into opportunities to enhance our educational environments. As we near the close of this chapter, I want to share some practical strategies to help you overcome these common hurdles. These are designed to guide you in navigating the complexities of tech integration by helping you leverage digital tools effectively. From securing funding to fostering a positive tech culture, these tips will equip you to lead your teams confidently and smoothly through the transition. Let's dive in to see how you can turn challenges into stepping stones for success!

- **Budget constraints:** Limited financial resources can hinder the adoption of advanced technological tools.
  - *Solutions*—Explore funding sources such as grants, partnerships with technology companies, and government programs. Examine and present the long-term benefits and cost savings of technological investments to secure budget allocations (Robinson et al., 2019).

- **Resistance to change:** Educators and administrators may be hesitant to adopt new technologies due to their comfort with existing methods or skepticism about the efficacy of new tools.
  - *Solutions*—Foster a positive attitude toward technology by involving educators in decision-making processes, highlighting successful case studies, and offering continuous support and training. Build commitment through collaboration and celebrating early successes (Robinson et al., 2019).

- **Training needs:** Effective integration of technology depends on comprehensive training and ongoing professional learning.
  - *Solutions*—Develop hands-on, relevant training programs aligned with teachers' daily tasks. Provide ongoing support and create a culture of collaborative learning where educators can share insights and troubleshoot challenges together (Robinson et al., 2019; Siyam, 2019).
- **Infrastructure gaps:** For my in-person school leaders, outdated hardware and insufficient internet access can limit the potential of technology in schools.
  - *Solutions*—Invest in upgraded infrastructure, including reliable internet and modern devices. Collaborate with local governments and private sectors to secure funding and resources to close infrastructure gaps (Robinson et al., 2019).
- **Data privacy concerns:** Concerns about data privacy and security can create hesitation in adopting new technologies, especially those involving sensitive student information.
  - *Solutions*—Establish and enforce strict data privacy policies to ensure compliance with regulations like the Family Educational Rights and Privacy Act (1974). Educate staff and parents about best practices for maintaining data security and privacy. Regularly review and update security protocols to address emerging threats (Robinson et al., 2019; Siyam, 2019).

 Voices From the Field

The following vignette is shared by Nicole, a dedicated special education teacher who integrates digital tools, assistive technology, and AI into her practice. Nicole's innovative approach to using these technologies in IEP data collection, parent communication, and UDL has not only enhanced her students' engagement and success but also streamlined her own workload.

Nicole's story reflects the central themes of this chapter: leveraging technology to address workload challenges, improve communication, and foster equitable learning opportunities. Her firsthand experience demonstrates how thoughtful implementation of digital tools can transform teaching practices, empowering both educators and students to thrive. Her insights provide a compelling case for school leaders to champion these tools in their schools to support retention, efficiency, and inclusive education.

DIGITAL IEP SOLUTIONS

In my experience as a special education teacher and case manager, utilizing digital tools, assistive technology, and AI has played a key role in my success. I have used these resources in my IEP data collection and parent communication, and I provide UDL opportunities in my classroom. By leveraging these tools, my stress level has decreased; my students are more engaged and eager to learn; and the families I work with can see their children's growth.

This past school year, I had the opportunity to take my once self-contained cohort of students into a general education biology classroom. I was apprehensive when I first heard of this initiative due to my students' reading, writing, and self-control skills. My students, who had a kindergarten reading and writing level, used speech-to-text tools to support their writing and text-to-speech tools to support their reading. After hours and a plethora of trial and error, I decided my favorite program was NaturalReader. My high school students were able to discreetly have an earbud in one ear and simply take a picture of whatever they needed to have read to them. We were able to be in the general education setting with support while maintaining their dignity, and we provided accommodations in the classroom while maintaining rigor. Digital tools helped me maintain accurate behavioral data for their self-control skills. I added the PBIS Rewards teacher app to my phone and gave them points for behaviors such as engagement and task completion.

In the beginning of my career, I utilized classic pencil-and-paper data collection techniques. The problem with that is I never had the time to create a graph using the data I recorded. I would look at the data and simply determine whether a student met the particular goal; however, parents want more! Most parents want to see the details of their child's growth. When I was an intern teacher, my classmate mentioned that she used Google Forms to track data, so that inspired me to use Microsoft Forms. Using Microsoft Forms, I could quickly track data on my phone, and when analyzing said data, I could create graphs, which my parents appreciated!

—Nicole Soto, High School Special Education Teacher and Case Manager, Washington State

Takeaway Tool Kit

The journey of integrating technology is truly about transforming the learning environment to make it more inclusive, efficient, and supportive for both educators and students. By thoughtfully considering the reflective questions in figure 5.1, you can begin to evaluate your current practices, identify areas for improvement, and develop strategic plans that aim to ensure the successful use of digital tools. I hope this reflective process will help you overcome barriers, embrace opportunities, and ultimately enhance the educational experience for all members of your school community.

Integrating technology into your practices requires thoughtful planning and a strategic approach to selecting appropriate tools to meet the diverse needs of your students and educators. Figure 5.2 (page 147) is a practical guide designed to guide you through some essential steps to consider when exploring and implementing digital tools into your educational programs. By following this list of guidelines, you can create a foundation for a seamless and effective integration process that enhances teaching, learning, and operational efficiency, ultimately fostering a more inclusive and supportive educational environment for your teachers and students.

Enhancing collaborative planning is necessary for advancing educational outcomes and effective resource sharing among educators, especially for the benefit of special education. Figure 5.3 (page 149) offers practical steps and tips for school leaders to leverage collaborative tools, streamline planning processes, and foster a culture of teamwork that supports inclusive and effective instruction.

Figure 5.4 (page 150) offers a briefly curated introductory resource list highlighting present-day technological resources. From tools that aim to facilitate effective communication and collaboration to those that offer robust assistive technologies and interactive learning experiences, these resources are designed to empower your educators and support their professional growth. Now, remember my focus is on the present day, and quite frankly, I look forward to the constant evolution of education and technology. So, as changes are made, one or more of the tools listed may be replaced or changed significantly.

Reflection Question	Your Answer	Action Steps
1. How are you currently integrating digital tools into your special education programs, and what successes and challenges have you experienced so far?		Identify specific digital tools that have been effective and expand their use across different classrooms.
2. In what ways have digital tools improved communication, documentation, and instructional planning within your school community?		Implement a unified digital platform for all communication and documentation to ensure consistency and ease of access.
3. How do you measure the impact of digital tools on reducing the administrative burden for special education teachers?		Conduct regular surveys and time-tracking studies to quantify time saved and identify areas for further improvement.
4. What strategies have you implemented to ensure that digital tools are accessible and effective for all your students?		Review and update accessibility features on all digital tools and provide training for staff on how to use those features effectively.
5. How do you support continuous professional development for teachers to enhance their proficiency with digital tools and help them effectively integrate those tools into their teaching practices?		Schedule regular professional development sessions focused on digital tools and their applications in special education.
6. How do you address resistance to technology adoption among staff, and what strategies have been most effective in overcoming these barriers?		Create a mentorship program where tech-savvy teachers support colleagues who are less comfortable with technology.
7. How do you ensure that digital tools and resources are used to create an inclusive and engaging learning environment for all students?		Develop and share a repository of engaging, inclusive lesson plans that utilize digital tools.

continued >

Figure 5.1: Empowering progress through reflection.

Reflection Question	Your Answer	Action Steps
8. What processes do you have in place to monitor and evaluate the effectiveness of technology integration in your special education programs?		Establish a committee to regularly review technology integration and its outcomes, and make adjustments as needed.
9. How do you plan to sustain and scale the use of digital tools in special education to continually improve educational outcomes and teacher satisfaction?		Develop a long-term technology plan that includes budgeting, training, and ongoing support for teachers.
10. What steps have you taken to involve all stakeholders—including parents, students, and support staff—in the integration of digital tools?		Host informational sessions and provide resources for parents and support staff to ensure they are comfortable with the digital tools being used.
11. How do you address budget constraints and secure funding to support the integration of technology in special education?		Apply for grants and collaborate with local businesses and organizations to secure additional funding.
12. In what ways do you use data to drive decision making and improve the use of digital tools in your special education programs?		Implement a data analytics tool to track student progress and identify areas where digital tools can be more effectively utilized.
13. What long-term goals do you have for integrating technology into your special education programs, and how do you plan to achieve them?		Set specific, measurable goals for technology integration and create a timeline for achieving those goals.
14. How do you celebrate and recognize the successes and effective practices of teachers who successfully integrate digital tools into their teaching?		Establish a recognition program to celebrate teachers' achievements in technology integration at staff meetings or through a school newsletter.

15. How can you create a more supportive and collaborative culture that embraces technology and innovation in special education?		Organize regular collaborative workshops where teachers can share their experiences and innovative practices using digital tools.
16. How do you ensure that ethical considerations such as data privacy and bias mitigation are addressed when implementing new technologies?		Develop and enforce a strict policy on data privacy and provide training on ethical technology use.
17. What additional resources or support do you need to further enhance the integration of digital tools in your special education programs?		Identify key resources needed, such as additional training, software, or hardware, and create a plan to acquire these resources.

Visit **go.SolutionTree.com/specialneeds** for a free reproducible version of this figure.

Assessment and Planning

1. Identify Needs and Goals
   - Determine the specific needs of your students, teachers, and overall educational program.
   - Define clear objectives for what you hope to achieve with the new technology.

   Example: "Our goal is to improve student engagement and provide more personalized learning experiences."

2. Conduct a Technology Audit
   - Assess existing technologies and identify gaps that the new tools will fill.

   Example: "We currently lack tools for real-time feedback and interactive learning."

Stakeholder Involvement

3. Gather Input From All Stakeholders
   - Involve teachers, students, parents, and administrators in the decision-making process.

   Example: "We will host focus groups or distribute surveys to gather input on technology needs and preferences."

4. Form a Technology Committee
   - Create a dedicated team to oversee the integration process.

   Example: "Our technology committee includes IT staff, teachers, and a parent representative."

continued >

Figure 5.2: Technology integration guide for school leaders.

Budget and Resources

5. Allocate Budget
   - Secure funding and allocate a budget for purchasing and maintaining new technology and training staff.

   Example: "We will apply for grants and explore partnerships with tech companies for funding."

6. Ensure Infrastructure Readiness
   - Verify that your school's infrastructure can support the new technology.

   Example: "We will upgrade our Wi-Fi network to handle increased traffic from new devices."

Professional Development

7. Plan Training Programs
   - Develop comprehensive training programs for teachers.

   Example: "We will schedule workshops and ongoing professional development sessions."

8. Establish Mentorship Opportunities
   - Pair tech-savvy teachers with those who need additional support.

   Example: "We will create a buddy system where experienced teachers mentor their peers."

Implementation

9. Pilot Programs
   - Start with a pilot program to test the new technology on a small scale.

   Example: "We will implement the new learning management system in one grade level first."

10. Gather Feedback and Make Adjustments
    - Collect feedback from the pilot program and make necessary adjustments.

    Example: "We will conduct surveys and hold feedback sessions to gather insights from the pilot program."

Monitoring and Evaluation

11. Track Progress and Impact
    - Use data and analytics to monitor the effectiveness of the new technology.

    Example: "We will use student performance data to assess the impact of the new interactive learning tools."

12. Regularly Review and Update
    - Continuously review the technology integration plan and update it based on feedback and advancements.

    Example: "We will hold quarterly review meetings to assess progress and make necessary adjustments."

*Visit **go.SolutionTree.com/specialneeds** for a free reproducible version of this figure.*

Leveraging Digital Tools, Assistive Technology, and AI   149

Step 1: Establish Clear Objectives
- Identify Shared Goals
  - Determine common objectives that the collaborative planning process aims to achieve.

Example: Improve student engagement and academic performance.
- Set Clear Expectations
  - Clarify the roles and responsibilities of each team member.

Example: Assign a lead coordinator for each subject area or project.

Step 2: Select Appropriate Collaborative Tools
- Choose Suitable Tools
  - Select tools that meet the needs of your team and planning activities.

Example: Use Google Workspace for document sharing, Trello for project management, and Slack for communication.
- Ensure Accessibility
  - Make sure all team members have access to and are comfortable using the selected tools.

Example: Provide training sessions on effectively using new tools.

Step 3: Organize and Share Resources
- Create a Shared Repository
  - Set up a central location for storing and sharing planning documents and resources.

Example: Use tools such as Google Drive or Microsoft OneDrive to create shared folders for lesson plans, schedules, and instructional materials.
- Maintain Up-to-Date Resources
  - Regularly update and organize shared resources to ensure they are current and easily accessible.

Example: Assign a team member to manage and update the repository monthly.

Step 4: Schedule Regular Collaborative Meetings
- Plan Regular Check-Ins
  - Schedule consistent meetings to discuss progress, challenges, and next steps.

Example: Hold weekly or biweekly planning meetings using videoconferencing tools like Zoom or Microsoft Teams.
- Encourage Open Dialogue
  - Foster an environment where team members feel comfortable sharing ideas and feedback.

Example: Use an agenda template to structure meetings and ensure all voices are heard.

Step 5: Monitor Progress and Adjust Plans
- Use Project Management Tools
  - Utilize tools like Asana or Trello to track the progress of collaborative planning activities.

continued >

Figure 5.3: Collaborative planning guide.

Example: Create boards and assign tasks with due dates to monitor ongoing projects.
- Adjust Plans as Needed
  - Be flexible and willing to modify plans based on feedback and changing needs.

Example: Regularly review and update plans during meetings to reflect on any necessary changes.

Step 6: Evaluate and Reflect
- Collect Feedback
  - Gather input from team members on the collaborative planning process and the tools used.

Example: Use surveys or feedback forms to collect insights from the team.
- Reflect and Improve
  - Analyze feedback and make improvements to the collaborative planning process.

Example: Hold a reflection meeting at the end of each term to discuss successes and areas for improvement.

Visit **go.SolutionTree.com/specialneeds** for a free reproducible version of this figure.

Communication Tools
- Google Classroom
  - Description: A free web service for schools that aims to simplify creating, distributing, and grading assignments in a paperless way
  - Features: Streamlined communication, document sharing, and integration with Google Workspace
  - Link: https://classroom.google.com
- Remind
  - Description: A communication platform that helps teachers send real-time messages to students and parents
  - Features: Text messaging, announcements, and individual messaging
  - Link: www.remind.com
- ClassDojo
  - Description: A classroom management tool that helps teachers improve student behavior and communicate more effectively with parents
  - Features: Behavior tracking, instant messaging, and photo and video sharing
  - Link: www.classdojo.com
- Seesaw
  - Description: A digital portfolio and communication platform for teachers, students, and families
  - Features: Student-driven portfolios, family engagement, and multimedia tools
  - Link: https://web.seesaw.me

- TalkingPoints
    - Description: A multilingual communication application that helps teachers communicate with non-English-speaking parents
    - Features: Two-way translation, message scheduling, and engagement tracking
    - Link: https://talkingpts.org

Collaboration and Project Management Tools
- Google Drive
    - Description: A file storage and synchronization service that allows users to store files in the cloud
    - Features: Document creation, sharing, and collaboration in real time
    - Link: https://google.com/drive
- Trello
    - Description: A web-based project management application that uses boards, lists, and cards
    - Features: Task management, collaboration, and workflow automation
    - Link: https://trello.com
- Microsoft Teams
    - Description: A collaboration platform that integrates with Office 365
    - Features: Chat messaging, videoconferencing, file sharing, and collaborative workspaces
    - Link: www.microsoft.com/en-us/microsoft-teams/group-chat-software
- Slack
    - Description: A messaging application for teams that brings all communication together in one place
    - Features: Channels, direct messaging, file sharing, and integration with other tools
    - Link: https://slack.com
- Padlet
    - Description: An online bulletin board where teachers and students can collaborate by posting notes, links, images, and videos
    - Features: Real-time updates, multimedia support, and customizable layouts
    - Link: https://padlet.com

Asynchronous Video Tools
- Loom
    - Description: A video messaging tool that allows users to record their screen, camera, and microphone
    - Features: Video recording, instant sharing, and viewer engagement tracking
    - Link: www.loom.com
- ScreenPal (formerly Screencast-O-Matic)
    - Description: A screen recording and video editing tool that is easy to use and accessible
    - Features: Screen recording, video editing, and direct sharing to platforms like YouTube
    - Link: https://screenpal.com

continued >

Figure 5.4: Introductory resource list.

- Edpuzzle
  - Description: A tool that allows teachers to make an interactive video of their lesson by adding questions and voice-over
  - Features: Video editing, interactive questions, and progress tracking
  - Link: https://edpuzzle.com
- Vidyard
  - Description: A video platform for businesses that offers educational solutions for creating and sharing instructional videos
  - Features: Video recording, sharing, and analytics
  - Link: www.vidyard.com/virtual-teaching

Assistive Technology Tools
- SpeechTexter
  - Description: A web-based dictation tool that allows users to create text documents using voice typing
  - Features: Real-time speech recognition and multi-language support
  - Link: www.speechtexter.com
- NaturalReader
  - Description: A text-to-speech software that converts written text into spoken words
  - Features: Multiple voices, adjustable reading speed, and support for various file formats
  - Link: www.naturalreaders.com
- Grammarly
  - Description: An AI-powered writing assistant that helps with grammar, spelling, and style improvements
  - Features: Grammar check, style suggestions, and plagiarism detection
  - Link: www.grammarly.com
- Ginger Software
  - Description: A tool that offers grammar and spelling checks, translation, and text-to-speech capabilities
  - Features: Grammar and spelling checks, a text reader, and translation
  - Link: www.gingersoftware.com
- Kurzweil 3000
  - Description: An assistive technology tool that provides reading, writing, and study support for diverse learners
  - Features: Text to speech, reading comprehension tools, and study aids
  - Link: www.kurzweil3000.com

Interactive Learning Tools
- Kahoot!
  - Description: A game-based learning platform that makes it easy to create, share, and play learning games or take trivia quizzes
  - Features: Interactive quizzes, real-time feedback, and engagement tools
  - Link: https://kahoot.com
- Quizlet
  - Description: A study tool that provides various study modes, including flash cards and games, to help students learn
  - Features: Flash cards, learning games, and study modes
  - Link: https://quizlet.com

- Nearpod
  - Description: An interactive learning tool that allows teachers to create presentations that can contain quizzes, polls, videos, and other multimedia elements
  - Features: Interactive lessons, real-time assessment, and student engagement tracking
  - Link: www.nearpod.com
- Pear Deck
  - Description: An interactive presentation tool used to engage students in individual and social learning
  - Features: Interactive slides, real-time feedback, and formative assessments
  - Link: www.peardeck.com
- Plickers
  - Description: A simple tool that lets teachers collect real-time formative assessment data without the need for student devices
  - Features: Instant feedback, easy-to-use assessment tool, and data collection
  - Link: www.plickers.com

Professional Development Tools
- Edpuzzle
  - Description: A platform that allows teachers to make an interactive video of their lesson by adding questions and voice-over
  - Features: Video editing, interactive questions, and progress tracking
  - Link: https://edpuzzle.com
- Common Sense Education
  - Description: A platform of free resources for educators to teach digital citizenship and integrate technology into the classroom
  - Features: Lesson plans, professional development, and technology integration strategies
  - Link: www.commonsense.org/education
- Google for Education: Teacher Center
  - Description: A platform that offers free training, resources, and certifications for educators to learn how to effectively use Google tools in the classroom
  - Features: Online courses, certifications, and classroom resources
  - Link: https://edu.google.com/for-educators/overview
- Coursera
  - Description: An online learning platform offering courses from top universities and companies, including many free courses for educators
  - Features: Professional development courses, certificates, and peer collaboration
  - Link: www.coursera.org
- Khan Academy
  - Description: A platform that offers free online courses, lessons, and practice in a wide range of subjects
  - Features: Instructional videos, practice exercises, and a personalized learning dashboard
  - Link: www.khanacademy.org

*Visit **go.SolutionTree.com/specialneeds** for a free reproducible version of this figure.*

Wrap-Up

As we conclude this chapter on leveraging technology to empower special education, I hope you notice the broader implications and practical applications of what we've discussed. Technology is not just a tool—it's a catalyst for transformation. When integrated thoughtfully, it can help you enhance operational efficiency, support teachers, and improve student outcomes. Eric Sheninger (2019) reminds us that technology's role in education goes beyond innovation—it can support us in reshaping school culture and strengthening collaboration.

The effective integration of technology requires deliberate planning, ongoing professional learning, and a collaborative mindset. Regular training and mentorship programs equip educators with the skills and confidence to embrace new tools while fostering a supportive culture of collaboration that encourages continuous learning and innovation.

Finally, remember that the journey of technology integration doesn't end with implementation. Regularly monitor and evaluate the impact of these tools on both student learning and teacher satisfaction. Use feedback and performance data to refine your strategies, ensuring they remain effective and aligned with your goals.

Technology holds the potential to revolutionize the educational experience. By embracing this opportunity with intentionality and purpose, you can create an environment where technology supports you in empowering your team and transforming learning for all.

Chapter Six

Optimizing Workload Management and Performance Improvement

Special educators are champions for our most vulnerable learners, tirelessly working to make certain that every student's unique needs are met. Yet, despite their dedication, they often find themselves battling against an unsupportive system, stretched thin by an overwhelming workload, and feeling undervalued. Before we dive deep here, I want to be clear that special education teachers are not the only teachers experiencing demanding workloads—four out of every five teachers report increased stress directly related to their school workload (Juniper Education, 2023). More than 50 percent of teachers report their workloads have an adverse effect on their mental and physical well-being, and over 65 percent of teachers contemplate leaving the profession entirely because of their workload (Juniper Education, 2023). While my focus in this chapter is centered on special educators, I believe it's important to highlight the widespread concern.

School systems were not historically designed to meet the needs of diverse learners; therefore, they were not designed around the needs of special education staff (Blad, 2024). This systemic disconnect too often leaves special educators scrambling to provide services and support with limited resources and recognition. Imagine trying to craft individualized lesson plans, manage behavioral supports, and handle extensive paperwork (Brunsting, Sreckovic, & Lane, 2014), all without adequate planning time or a seat at the table for crucial discussions on topics such as curriculum and resources. This is the daily reality for many special education teachers. Why does this matter? Overwhelming workloads contribute to job dissatisfaction, which is a leading factor in high turnover for special educators. Special educators are more likely to stay in schools when working conditions and school culture are positive (Ansley et al., 2019).

In this chapter, I will guide you through actionable and practical strategies to collaboratively optimize teachers' workloads and challenge you to reimagine your performance improvement approach. This chapter is not meant to be exhaustive; I hope its content ignites creativity and innovation beyond these pages and inspires you to continue learning. My goal with this chapter is to share my knowledge and experiences and provide strategies and guides to partner with you in your support of special educators.

First, we will explore the concept of transitioning from a caseload approach to a workload approach, a method that acknowledges the full scope of a teacher's responsibilities and, I hope, leads to better service delivery and increased job satisfaction. Then, we will unpack a transformative approach to performance improvement that features a positive mindset and the creation of collaborative plans for success. By the end of this chapter, you will have gained actionable insights necessary to optimize workload management and transform performance improvement processes, adding to your school leadership toolbox.

Workload Management

Now, let's turn our focus to one of the most significant stressors for special educators: workload management. Special education teachers are charged with particularly demanding work responsibilities, and it's not due to the students (Blad, 2024). By addressing and optimizing their workload, we can help alleviate some of the pressures they face, thereby enhancing their job satisfaction and effectiveness and, ultimately, improving outcomes for the students they so passionately serve.

You may be reading this text and wondering, "What are these responsibilities you're talking about?" First, let me be clear: I do not claim to know the organizational structure of all schools nor the lived experiences of all teachers and administrators. However, given my experiences, the experiences others have shared, and my continuous efforts to study the field, I'd like to highlight a few common aspects of a special education teacher's role. These responsibilities are not all exclusive to special educators.

To truly address the pressing concerns of workload management, we must first develop a shared understanding of the unique and multifaceted responsibilities special educators shoulder daily. Their responsibilities extend far beyond the classroom to encompass delivering individualized instruction, being a nurturing spirit for their students, administering behavioral interventions, complying with legal requirements, and building relationships with families and colleagues. These responsibilities require not only expertise but also resilience, collaboration, and unwavering commitment. As school leaders, recognizing and appreciating this complexity are the first steps toward offering meaningful support.

The following points outline some of the most significant demands placed on special education teachers. By first reviewing these, we can begin to identify where strategic support and leadership can make a transformative impact.

- **Individualized instruction:** As school leaders, it's crucial to understand the monumental task special education teachers face in developing and implementing IEPs. These programs are not one-size-fits-all and legally are exempt from being such; rather, they require individualization, regular assessments and monitoring, specific goal setting, and continuous adaptation to meet the unique needs of each student (Ansley et al., 2019). Historically, special educators were viewed as entirely responsible for the educational progress of students with disabilities, and while we've come a long way in North America, continued progress toward equity-centered beliefs and pedagogy is necessary.

- **Behavioral interventions:** Another significant part of their role is supporting diverse behavior tendencies through formal Behavior Intervention Plans (BIPs). These involve not just monitoring and supporting student behavior but also collecting data and working closely with staff to ensure consistent and effective approaches (Ansley et al., 2019; Brunsting et al., 2014). This process demands a high level of expertise in behavioral strategies and a commitment to fostering a positive learning environment, and is often an area educators seek support in.

- **Relationship management:** Managing relationships with guardians is a complex and essential aspect of their role. Teachers are legally mandated to update guardians on their child's progress, involve them in the IEP process, and address any concerns they might have. These requirements demand exceptional—or at least effective—communication skills and the ability to navigate sensitive conversations, all while striving to maintain a collaborative and supportive relationship with the family. One critical dimension of managing custodial relationships in special education is the need for conflict resolution skills. Conflicts may arise due to differing perspectives on a student's needs, progress, or the approaches being used. Teachers are pressured to be adept at mediating these conflicts, understanding the parents' concerns, and striving to move forward as agreeably as possible. This skill set is particularly important in special education, where guardians are sometimes more intensely involved in their child's education and may have strong opinions on what they believe is best. This includes understanding any cultural, socioeconomic, and personal factors that influence the parents' views and concerns. Being empathetic and respectful of these factors can help build trust and cooperation, making it easier to work together in the student's best interests.

- **Complex legalities:** Another layer of complexity in fostering healthy family relationships in special education is navigating the legal parameters that guide these programs. Special education is governed by laws such as the Individuals with Disabilities Education Act (2004), which aims to ensure all students with disabilities receive *free appropriate public education* (FAPE; Individuals with Disabilities Education Act, 2004) tailored to their individual needs. Teachers must be careful that all communications and actions comply with these legal requirements to protect the rights of the student and maintain transparency with guardians about what services and supports are provided. By addressing these areas—conflict resolution, case sensitivity, and legal compliance—you, as a school leader, can support special education teaching teams in effectively navigating family relationships. Providing training and resources in these areas can help teachers feel more confident and competent in their family interactions, ultimately contributing to a more supportive and effective educational environment for their students.

- **Administrative work:** Last, but certainly not least, is the considerable administrative burden and extensive paperwork. Special education teachers often serve as case managers for their students and must meticulously maintain detailed records of student progress, complete comprehensive IEP documentation, and ensure compliance with numerous legal and regulatory requirements (Brunsting et al., 2014). This extensive paperwork can be overwhelming and often detracts from precious time and energy for direct instruction and meaningful interactions with their students and colleagues. Picture a teacher, passionate and dedicated yet buried under piles of documentation, striving to keep up with the bureaucratic demands while still trying to be present for their students. Recall chapter four's focus on collaborative IEP processes. This is the reality for many in the field of special education. The sheer volume of administrative tasks can lead to significant stress and burnout, making it difficult for teachers to maintain high standards of care for and attention to their students' diverse learning needs. Moreover, the constant pressure to meet legal and regulatory standards can leave teachers feeling like they are always playing catch-up and never quite able to give their full attention to the classroom, where it is needed most. It's a balancing act that requires incredible skill, knowledge, resilience, and diligence, yet without adequate support, it can quickly become untenable.

As a school leader, I am calling on you to recognize this burden and take proactive steps to equitably lighten the load. This means deepening your understanding of special educators' unique roles, creating space to seek and value their input, advocating for streamlined administrative processes, providing adequate instructional and administrative planning time, and ensuring special education staff have access to the resources and support they need to manage their workloads effectively.

Strategies for Optimizing Workloads

Now that you have an overview of the diverse responsibilities of many special education teachers, let's explore actionable and practical strategies that can aid you in optimizing teachers' workloads. My hope is that you and your team leverage these strategies to foster a nurturing and efficient environment, with the intent to positively contribute to job satisfaction and effectiveness. As I mentioned before, studies have found a significant link between teacher burnout and their job satisfaction (Emery & Vandenberg, 2010; Robinson et al., 2019; Shen et al., 2015), with burnout being the leading cause of their leaving the profession entirely. Remember, when considering the use of any strategy, it is vital you equitably examine the uniqueness of your school context.

Transitioning From a Caseload Approach to a Workload Approach

Shifting from a traditional caseload approach to a workload approach can make a significant difference. The workload approach considers all the tasks a teacher performs, not just a count of students on their caseload and the "minutes" for each one. Special education teachers are required to manage several roles (Robinson et al., 2019), which means we must consider the number of students on a teacher's caseload, the diverse learning needs, the service-learning models to be addressed (consultative, direct instruction, co-teaching, solo teaching, and so on), instructional planning, IEP documentation, and communication with parents and colleagues—to name a few. This method acknowledges the full scope of a teacher's responsibilities, which can lead to better service delivery and teacher effectiveness (White, 2024). By optimizing the workload, you can better align resources with the realities of special educators' roles. As Melissa White (2024) highlights, transitioning to this model enables educators to focus on quality over quantity, which fosters a more sustainable and supportive work environment. By recognizing and addressing the comprehensive nature of their work, we can create systems that prioritize both educator well-being and student success.

To implement this workload approach I describe, I encourage you to begin by conducting a thorough analysis of each teacher's responsibilities. This could be an area of focus on a needs assessment. Consider revisiting chapter 2 (page 37) if you'd like a refresher. To do this, gather detailed input from your special education teachers about their daily tasks and challenges; use this information to develop a more holistic understanding of their workload; and reallocate resources to ensure that tasks are distributed equitably. This might involve hiring additional support staff to assist with administrative duties or ensuring that other support roles are utilized effectively. Additionally, adjust scheduling to allow for more flexible time management to ensure that teachers have adequate time for planning, instruction, and administrative tasks. Regularly review and adjust the workload distribution to maintain balance and address any emerging issues promptly. By considering these strategies, you are working to ensure special education teachers have the time and resources they need to focus on delivering high-quality education to their students.

Promoting Collaborative Planning

Fostering a culture of collaborative planning is a game changer for educators committed to the learning of all students (Muhammad, 2024). I am sure you've recognized the collaborative theme of this book, and it continues to be essential in this final chapter. Encouraging special education teachers to collaborate with general and other educators, and vice versa, promotes a shared commitment to student success. Recurring cycles of inquiry that focus on data-driven decisions help distribute the workload more equitably, facilitate the sharing of best practices, and ensure a unified approach to students' needs. This collaborative environment can alleviate individual stress while targeting the needs of students (Juniper Education, 2023). By creating a culture where collaboration is valued and routine, schools can enhance both teacher satisfaction and student outcomes.

To effectively foster a collaborative planning culture, start by scheduling regular, dedicated time for joint planning sessions or digital communication pathways. Ensure that these sessions are structured and purposeful, with clear agendas or prompts that focus on student data, instructional strategies, and problem solving. As a school leader, it's crucial to clearly communicate your expectations for these types of opportunities. Describe the objectives and outcomes you expect, such as data analysis, lesson planning, and strategy sharing. To ensure that collaborative planning time is used effectively and not misused, regularly inspect and review the outputs of these sessions. This oversight helps maintain focus and productivity, preventing time from being wasted and aiming to ensure that the collaborative efforts align with the mission of optimizing workloads.

Encourage open communication and mutual respect among team members to promote an environment where every voice is heard and valued. Provide opportunities for professional development that focus on collaborative skills and effective teamwork. By implementing these strategies and maintaining clear expectations and accountability, you can build a strong foundation for collaboration that benefits both teachers and students.

There are various forms of collective pedagogy that I have addressed throughout this book. Figure 6.1 provides an additional quick guide you might leverage to host collaborative planning sessions to support teacher workloads.

Quick Guide for Collaborative Planning Sessions

This template is designed to help structure and guide collaborative planning sessions. Print or share digitally to encourage real-time input from all participants. At the end of each session, save the completed template for follow-up and accountability.

Session Date: _____

Participants: _____

Facilitator (if applicable): _____

Session Agenda

Objective of the Session
What are we aiming to achieve in this session?
Examples: Analyze student data, plan lessons, address classroom challenges, share strategies

Data Analysis
What data are we reviewing, and what insights can we gather from that data?
Examples: Assessment results, attendance trends, behavior logs
Data Source:

Key Insights:

Lesson Planning
Which lessons or units are we planning collaboratively?
Examples: Grade 6 science unit, interventions for struggling readers
Focus Area:

Ideas or Strategies:

Optimizing Workload Management and Performance Improvement

Strategy Sharing
What best practices or strategies are participants contributing?
Examples: Co-teaching techniques, classroom management tips
Shared Strategies:

Planned Applications:

Action Items and Task Assignments
What needs to be done, and who is responsible for each task?
Examples: Create differentiated lesson plans, update student IEP goals

Task	Person Responsible	Due Date

Follow-Up Checklist
What do we need to revisit or follow up on in the next session?
Examples: Check lesson plan implementation, review progress on action items

Reflection and Feedback
How did this session go? What worked well, and what could be improved for future sessions?

Integration With Digital Formats
To enhance accessibility and collaboration, consider adapting this template into a shared digital format, such as a Google Doc, Microsoft Teams form, or shared platform like Trello or Asana. Doing so allows participants to contribute asynchronously and track progress in real time.

Figure 6.1: Quick guide for collaborative planning sessions.
*Visit **go.SolutionTree.com/specialneeds** for a free reproducible version of this figure.*

Implementing Regular Feedback and Support

Regular feedback opportunities with special education teachers are essential for understanding the specific challenges they face and providing timely support. These interactions allow you to gain valuable insights into their daily struggles and triumphs, creating opportunities to address concerns promptly and effectively. Empathy-driven conversations and a focus on teacher well-being can significantly enhance job satisfaction and reduce burnout, ultimately leading to a more positive and productive school environment (Nichols, 2024). Who doesn't want that?

To implement effective, relevant, and timely feedback and support, establish a routine schedule for connecting with your team. These sessions should be frequent enough for you to be a thought partner on the teachers' ongoing work and to address any concerns, but not be so frequent that they become burdensome. During these meetings, actively listen to your teachers' feedback and show genuine interest and empathy for their experiences. Use these engagements to identify specific challenges and collaboratively develop solutions. When giving feedback, provide it in a way that is constructive, actionable, and focused on professional growth. Additionally, foster a supportive atmosphere where teachers feel comfortable sharing their thoughts and concerns without fear of judgment. Recognize and celebrate their achievements regularly to boost morale and motivation. By cultivating an environment of continuous support and open communication, you can help your special education teachers feel valued, understood, and empowered to succeed.

Training in Time Management Techniques

Many teachers find themselves overwhelmed by the multitude of tasks they need to juggle daily and could benefit from guidance in managing their time more effectively. Training on how to prioritize tasks, set realistic goals, and utilize time-saving tools can empower teachers to manage their workload more efficiently. Encouraging the use of digital tools such as calendar applications, task management software, and automated reminders can help teachers stay organized and reduce the cognitive load of remembering numerous tasks.

To support teachers in developing strong time management skills, start by offering targeted professional learning workshops focused on effective time management strategies. These sessions can cover essential topics such as task prioritization, goal setting, and the use of digital tools to streamline daily activities. Ensure the professional learning experiences include hands-on training that permits teachers to experiment with different techniques and find what works best for them, as well as opportunities to apply the knowledge they're learning. Encourage the adoption of digital tools to help teachers stay organized and on track. Create a culture where teachers feel comfortable seeking guidance and support in managing their time. Regularly review and discuss time management practices during staff meetings to allow teachers to share their experiences and learn from each other.

I would be remiss if I didn't mention an equally important part of your role as it relates to management, and that is for you and your leadership team to consistently be mindful of your teachers' workload. Be careful not to assign tasks that are unmanageable, as that would undercut the purpose of lessening teachers' overwhelm. By equipping your teachers with the skills and tools they need to manage their time effectively, you can help reduce their stress and enhance their ability to focus on delivering high-quality instruction to their students.

Leveraging Technology and Software

Technology has the power to transform the way educators manage their responsibilities, especially in the demanding field of special education. While we dove into the broader applications of technology in chapter 5 (page 123), this section zeroes in on how you can leverage digital tools to specifically support workload optimization for special education teachers.

Remember the myriad responsibilities special educators face: crafting individualized lesson plans, managing IEPs, documenting progress, and fostering communication with parents and colleagues. Each of these tasks is essential but time-consuming. By integrating user-friendly technology solutions into these processes, school leaders can alleviate much of this burden, freeing teachers to focus on their core mission—teaching and supporting students.

Research underscores the efficacy of technology in streamlining administrative tasks and enhancing efficiency. For instance, platforms that consolidate IEP creation, student progress tracking, and parent communication into a single interface have been shown to reduce teachers' workload significantly while improving job satisfaction (Robinson et al., 2019). These tools not only save valuable time but also help ensure legal compliance and consistency in documentation.

The following are strategies for implementing technology effectively.

- **Assess needs first:** Every school's context is unique, and so are its challenges. Start by collaborating with your special education team to identify their most pressing needs. Are they overwhelmed with documentation? Struggling to track progress? In need of better communication tools? Use their input to inform your choice of software.

- **Select comprehensive platforms:** Look for platforms that integrate multiple functionalities, such as IEP management, data analysis, and parent communication. Tools like iTrack, Frontline Special Ed and Interventions (formerly IEP Direct), or other widely used education management systems can centralize tasks, making processes more efficient.

- **Provide thorough training:** Even the best software is only effective if users know how to navigate it. Organize professional learning sessions to help teachers develop confidence in using new tools. Training should be ongoing, with opportunities for refreshers and advanced feature exploration.

- **Collect regular feedback and adapt accordingly:** After implementation, gather teacher feedback to identify challenges and areas for improvement. Use this feedback to refine processes and provide additional support. This iterative approach ensures any new technology remains a tool for empowerment rather than a source of frustration.

- **Integrate technology into collaborative workflows:** Encourage teachers to use technology not only for administrative tasks but also for collaborative planning and communication. Shared digital platforms for lesson planning, real-time feedback, and resource sharing can streamline collaboration, enhance team productivity, and reduce duplication of efforts. For you online school leaders, leveraging technology is your whole world!

I encourage you to cultivate a mindset that embraces technology as a partner in teaching. School leaders play a pivotal role in setting this tone. Celebrate small wins, such as time saved or improved parent engagement, to demonstrate the tangible benefits of these tools. Highlight success stories within your team to build buy-in and confidence. Technology can be a pathway to empowerment. Tools that automate tedious processes allow teachers to reclaim time and energy, which they can then channel into high-impact activities like differentiated instruction, student engagement, and professional growth. Don't be mistaken: The same tools that revolutionize online learning environments can enhance in-person practices to make them more efficient and accessible for everyone involved. By leveraging technology thoughtfully, you can create an ecosystem where efficiency and support coexist, allowing teachers to focus on what truly matters—meeting the diverse needs of their students.

While this chapter explores workload optimization through various lenses, technology offers a unique and powerful avenue to reimagine how we support special education teachers. As you reflect on these insights, consider revisiting chapter 5 (page 123) for a broader perspective on digital integration and brainstorming ways to tailor those strategies specifically to your team's workload challenges.

Providing Ongoing Professional Learning

Research describes the importance of equipping teachers with practical skills and tools that help them manage their diverse responsibilities more effectively. Workshops on the areas we've discussed—such as time management, stress reduction techniques, and the use of educational technology—can make a significant difference. Additionally, training on collaboration and communication can enhance teamwork and reduce the isolation special education teachers often feel, thereby improving their overall job satisfaction and effectiveness (Robinson et al., 2019).

School leaders, here's a strategy that specifically applies to your leadership development. You and your leadership cabinet must take time to assess your own needs for development. You may need to engage in training that addresses the basics of special education laws, effective instructional strategies for diverse learners, the unique challenges special education teachers face, and so on. This will enhance your and your leadership team's capacity to effectively supervise and support special education staff (National Association of Secondary School Principals, 2021).

Offering Leadership Support

Providing strong leadership support is crucial for alleviating the workload of special education teachers. Effective leadership involves more than just administrative assistance—it requires enhancing your own capacity and creating an environment where teachers feel valued, supported, and empowered. Creating a supportive work environment is foundational to any workload optimization strategy. This involves providing the necessary resources and training and fostering a school culture that values and respects the contributions of special education teachers.

To provide impactful leadership support and create a supportive work environment, start by establishing regular, open lines of communication with your special education teachers. This may seem small, but it's mighty! You can achieve this through scheduled check-ins, feedback opportunities, and an open-door policy that encourages teachers to voice their concerns and suggestions. Clearly articulate your expectations and provide constructive feedback to help teachers meet their goals. Create a culture that celebrates successes, provides emotional support, and promotes collaboration among staff. Recognize and address the unique challenges special education teachers face and ensure they feel valued and respected within the school community.

Regularly review and adjust the workload distribution to maintain balance and address any emerging issues promptly. By fostering a supportive environment and providing strong leadership, you can create a positive and empowering atmosphere that enables special education teachers to thrive. This approach not only benefits the teachers but also positively impacts student outcomes, creating a more dynamic and supportive educational environment.

Leadership support doesn't end with creating an empowering environment—it also extends into how we approach performance improvement. Just as workload optimization benefits from thoughtful, collaborative leadership, performance improvement requires a mindset shift away from punitive measures and toward constructive, growth-oriented strategies.

This next section challenges traditional perceptions of Performance Improvement Plans (PIPs) and encourages a reimagined process that prioritizes professional growth, empathy, and shared accountability. By fostering a culture where improvement is seen as an opportunity rather than a consequence, leaders can create pathways for both teacher success and student achievement.

Let's explore how rethinking these processes can transform the way we support and develop our educators.

Supportive Performance Improvement With Collaborative Success Plans

Traditionally, PIPs have been viewed as punitive measures that create a climate of defensiveness, resentment, and anxiety among teachers. This approach can be counterproductive to the supposed purpose of this process, which is to create and implement a plan that targets performance improvement. Here, I challenge you to reflect on your current processes. In *Getting Teacher Evaluation Right*, Darling-Hammond (2013) emphasizes the importance of designing teacher evaluation systems that prioritize professional growth over punitive measures. The goal should be to help teachers develop their skills, enhance their effectiveness, and feel valued as professionals. By shifting from punitive measures to a supportive growth model, we can foster a more positive and encouraging environment that promotes continuous improvement and professional satisfaction (Network for Educator Effectiveness, n.d., 2022).

Before we continue, take a moment to reflect on the following ten questions about your current performance improvement process. Perhaps you are a new school leader, or you are new to the role at your campus and do not have experience with such a process. If that's the case, I encourage you to connect with someone who has experience directly working with teachers on a documented pathway to performance improvement and reflect together.

1. What is your current process for targeting areas necessary for teachers to improve?
2. Under what circumstances is this process most often initiated (for example, after a formal evaluation, when a pattern of poor performance persists for too long, after disciplinary action has been issued, and so on)?
3. Is there a process for teachers to initiate such an improvement plan?
4. Are teachers invited to the improvement process with the opportunity to decline, or is it always initiated as a required process?
5. In your experience, what reactions do teachers have to the initiation of your process?
6. In your experience, how successful is your process in positively contributing to teacher performance? Do teachers often resign as a result? Is their work performance enhanced?

7. Take a moment to reflect on your attitude and mindset throughout the improvement process.
    - Did you take time to understand the unique challenges and circumstances the teachers faced?
    - What were your initial thoughts and feelings when you initiated the PIP process?
    - How do you currently view the PIP process?
8. What resources and supports have you offered during the process?
9. How have you involved your teachers in the goal-setting stage?
10. Did you take time to celebrate progress and achievements?

The attitudes and beliefs you bring to performance improvement can mean the difference between a teacher feeling supported and encouraged or overwhelmed and discouraged. Let's unpack the transformative power of a leadership mindset rooted in empathy, collaboration, and a commitment to professional growth. This perspective reframes the way we address performance improvement and reimagines it as an opportunity to cultivate a culture of excellence and mutual respect.

Cultivating a Leadership Mindset

The attitudes and mindsets of school leaders significantly influence the success of performance improvement processes. Leaders who approach these plans with empathy, understanding, effective strategies, and a genuine desire to support their teachers can significantly impact outcomes (Darling-Hammond, 2013). A positive mindset from leaders can transform the way teachers perceive performance improvement, turning it from a dreaded obligation into a welcomed opportunity for growth. I am calling on you to adopt a collaborative and supportive attitude, demonstrating you are an ally in your teachers' professional journeys rather than an enforcer of rigid standards (Taylor & Tyler, n.d.).

Adopting a positive mindset and implementing effective strategies do not guarantee performance improvement. I'd be remiss if I didn't acknowledge that our fellow teachers have a crucial role to play in the process; however, that isn't the purpose of this chapter. My intention here is to inform and guide you in ways I hope impact your support for teachers. I hope to ignite reflection, redirection, rethinking, and celebration. To bridge the gap between traditional PIPs and a more collaborative and supportive approach that ditches the punitive style, consider implementing Collaborative Success Plans (CSPs). Informed by my firsthand experiences and a review of the literature, CSPs are my approach to performance improvement in which school leaders create plans designed to prevent the need for formal PIPs or to transform the mindset when entering that stage. CSPs focus on building partnerships among teachers and administrators and emphasize collaborative goal setting, continuous feedback, and tailored professional development. By focusing on supportive growth and continuous improvement, we can foster a culture of excellence and collaboration in our schools (Network for Educator Effectiveness, n.d., 2022; Taylor & Tyler, n.d.).

The mindset and attitude with which you address ongoing development can significantly influence the success of your team. When you approach performance processes with empathy, understanding, and a genuine desire to support your teachers, you can create a more positive and productive atmosphere. Transforming performance improvement from a punitive experience into a collaborative and empowering journey fosters a culture of growth and development (Darling-Hammond, 2013). Who doesn't want that?

Begin by reflecting on your attitudes toward performance improvement. Consider the guiding questions I provided earlier in this chapter. Explore how you can be more empathetic and encouraging.

Transforming Performance Improvement Into Success Plans

Next, I present key insights and strategies that are essential elements of CSPs. (You can find the supporting tool, the "Collaborative Success Plan (CSP) Template" in figure 6.3, page 181.) My goal here is not to increase the number of documented plans that are maintained at your school; I know there is a fair share of those currently existing. Rather, my goal is to support you in reimagining the already existing process of targeting improvement in teacher performance; whether you refer to this process as a PIP is not the focus. I intend for the following insights and strategies to guide you in developing and executing practices that foster a collaborative and supportive approach to teacher improvement.

Supporting teacher development should be an ongoing work habit, regardless of whether you use a CSP process. The following elements have the potential to contribute greatly to how your teachers are supported and to their ongoing professional development. You and your team might even consider partnering with all teachers near the start of the school year to jointly craft success plans. In this case, everyone can have a customized success plan. Consider how this could benefit your professional development plans for the school year. Whichever route you decide to take, keep these key elements in mind.

Clear Purpose and Collaborative Goals

Clarifying the purpose of performance improvement and ensuring a shared understanding among all involved are crucial. When teachers understand the intent and the need to identify areas of growth and plan for development, they are more likely to engage positively and collaboratively. Clearly communicate the purpose of engaging in a success plan, provide an opportunity for your teacher to ask clarifying questions, and reiterate the purpose to accomplish shared understanding. It is that simple.

From the onset, collectively crafting success plans with your teachers is critical to its success. After all, it is their success we are working toward. Allow teachers the opportunity to craft goals based on their needs and sincerely consider incorporating goals they've identified into their plan. Integrating teacher empowerment and autonomy into this process is most conducive to success and is essential for fostering a sense of ownership and accountability (Criss, Konrad, Alber-Morgan, & Brock, 2024; Darling-Hammond, 2013).

My favorite part about collaborative goal setting is emphasizing that it's critically important for this element to be driven by data. If your teachers have identified one or more goals, ask yourself, "How do we know this goal is necessary?" When collectively crafting goals, use data to identify areas for improvement, and don't forget to highlight the areas of strength indicated in the data. Strengths can be an incredible leveraging tool in the process of improvement. And last, but certainly not least, make SMART goals (Conzemius & O'Neill, 2014).

Transparent Implementation Process

Transparency is non-negotiable in this process. For feedback to be truly impactful, it must be immediate, specific, and consistent. Delaying feedback, such as by only discussing performance during scheduled check-ins, undermines the ongoing, authentic nature that CSPs aim to foster. CSPs should transcend mere documentation—they should become a lived experience of continuous professional growth where you, as a school leader, are an active partner in supporting the teacher's success journey. Clear understanding and communication of roles and responsibilities are crucial in achieving this transparency.

The following strategies will foster a transparent implementation approach to success plans.

- Clearly identify and communicate the roles of everyone involved in the CSP. Outline specific actions to be taken by the teacher, yourself as the school leader, and any other support personnel. This aims to ensure all parties understand their contributions to the teacher's growth journey.

- Provide feedback immediately after observing a teaching practice relevant to the CSP, whether it is through classroom visits, email reviews, or conversations. Feedback should not be reserved solely for scheduled check-ins. By giving timely feedback, you reinforce the actions needed for improvement and demonstrate your ongoing support (Criss et al., 2024; Darling-Hammond, 2013).

- Use visual aids to enhance the understanding and retention of feedback. These could include video clips from classroom visits, email exchanges, or checklist evaluations from recent observations. Visual presentations, combined with verbal feedback, make the feedback process more tangible and actionable for teachers.

- Identify the resources needed to support the teacher's goals and set clear timelines for when these resources will be provided. Additionally, specify the support that will accompany these resources, such as training sessions or mentoring. By doing so, you ensure that teachers have the necessary tools and support to succeed within a structured time frame.

Continuous Progress Monitoring

Regularly measuring and discussing progress toward goals during feedback sessions significantly improves teacher performance. This ongoing evaluation helps maintain focus and make necessary adjustments, ensuring that teachers remain on track to meet their objectives. By continuously monitoring progress, both teachers and administrators can identify areas of improvement and celebrate successes, fostering a culture of continuous growth and support (Criss et al., 2024; Network for Educator Effectiveness, n.d., 2022).

Establish a routine of biweekly or monthly progress review meetings where teachers and administrators discuss progress toward set goals, and use data-tracking tools to monitor progress and identify areas needing improvement. (For a simple, transparent spreadsheet template that I developed to monitor progress toward goals during these meetings, see the "CSP Simple Progress Monitoring Tracker" in figure 6.4, page 182.) During these sessions, encourage teachers to reflect and provide their own insights. This practice not only promotes self-awareness and accountability but also empowers teachers to take ownership of their professional development. Additionally, ensure that all feedback and progress are thoroughly documented in a transparent and accessible manner. This documentation should serve as a reference point for both teachers and administrators, helping to maintain a clear understanding of the teacher's development over time. It should be constructive and focused on growth rather than punishment. Implement the following strategies to enhance continuous progress monitoring.

- Schedule monthly, biweekly, or weekly review meetings, depending on the need, to discuss progress toward goals. These meetings should provide a structured opportunity for both teachers and administrators to reflect on achievements and identify areas for improvement.

- Encourage teachers to engage in self-reflection during progress review meetings. This practice helps teachers become more self-aware and take responsibility for their growth. Provide guiding questions or prompts to facilitate meaningful self-reflection.

- Document all feedback and progress discussions transparently and accessibly. This documentation should include details of the progress on SMART goals, feedback given, and any agreed-on actions. It serves as a valuable reference for continuous improvement and future discussions, with the intended goal of tracking the teacher's development journey. How else will you determine success? On page 182, I share a tracker I created and used when facilitating this process.

- Make timely adjustments based on the progress reviews. If certain strategies are not yielding the desired results, be flexible and willing to modify the approach. This agility ensures that teachers receive the support they need to succeed.

Recognition and Rewards

Recognizing and rewarding teachers for their efforts and achievements can boost morale, motivation, and job satisfaction. Positive reinforcement encourages continuous improvement and reinforces desired behaviors. Implement a recognition method that highlights and rewards teachers' successes and contributions. This could include awards, public acknowledgments, professional growth opportunities, and other incentives. Celebrate both small and significant achievements to maintain high levels of motivation and engagement.

Tips From the Top

The following are some top tips that reflect our discussion in this chapter. Here, I aim to further support your next steps in optimizing workload management and ensuring your performance improvement processes are effective and sustainable. Remember to walk the walk, model what you preach, and always inspect what you expect.

- **Lead by example:** Set the tone for a supportive and collaborative environment. Show empathy, actively listen, and demonstrate a commitment to professional growth. Your actions will inspire your team to follow suit!

- **Prioritize ongoing professional learning:** Invest in ongoing professional development tailored to the specific needs of your special education teachers. I cannot say this enough. Focus on areas such as time management, stress reduction, and instructional strategies. This, among other behaviors, shows you value their growth and development. Remember to involve your teachers in your training and support planning stages.

- **Use data to drive workload optimization and teacher development:** Utilize data to drive your decisions. I cannot emphasize this enough. Use both quantitative and qualitative data to gain a comprehensive understanding of each teacher's responsibilities and performance. Quantitative data, such as student performance metrics and teacher time logs, provide measurable insights into workload distribution and areas requiring support. Qualitative feedback gathered through classroom observations, teacher surveys, and feedback sessions offers valuable context and helps identify specific challenges and strengths.

- **Foster a culture of collaboration:** Encourage collaboration that promotes a unified approach to addressing students' needs.

- **Recognize and celebrate success:** Create a recognition program to celebrate the achievements and contributions of your special education teachers. Do not underestimate the power of positive affirmation and recognition in fostering a positive work environment, ultimately contributing to productivity.

- **Encourage self-reflection:** Promote a culture of self-reflection among your teachers by modeling this practice and making time for it during your meetings. Encourage them to regularly reflect on their practices, identify areas for improvement, and set personal goals. Self-reflection fosters a sense of ownership and accountability.

- **Provide emotional support:** Recognize the emotional labor involved in special education teaching and provide appropriate support. This might include access to counseling services, stress management workshops, and a supportive network of colleagues. Addressing emotional well-being can help reduce burnout and improve job satisfaction.

Voices From the Field

The following vignette is shared by Christina, a dedicated school building principal serving in the top performing school district in Arizona who exemplifies the transformative power of empathetic and collaborative leadership. As a champion for special education, Christina has worked tirelessly to address the systemic challenges highlighted in this chapter: overwhelming workloads, limited resources, and the undervaluing of special educators. Through her leadership, she has cultivated an environment that empowers teachers, optimizes workloads, and prioritizes inclusive practices.

I've had the privilege of witnessing Christina's educational journey for over a decade, not only as a colleague and friend but also as a partner in advancing the work of supporting special educators. Her commitment to building capacity, fostering teacher leadership, and transforming challenges into opportunities offers an inspiring blueprint for leaders looking to make a lasting impact in their schools.

BUILDING CAPACITY

As a school leader, I recognized that it was imperative that I build capacity around special education to ensure the needs of all students were being met, as well as empathize and partner with special education teachers. To achieve this, I embarked on a journey to deepen my understanding of special education. Attending conferences and workshops on topics like special education law and equitable practices allowed me to build a solid pedagogical foundation.

Simultaneously, I fostered relationships with special education professionals. Actively participating in IEP meetings, attending and facilitating weekly team gatherings, and asking thoughtful questions helped me gain insights into the policies and practices affecting our most vulnerable students. Collaborating closely with special education teachers allowed me to establish trust, express appreciation for their expertise, and retain highly effective educators. Through my growth and commitment to supporting special education, I discovered the importance of optimizing workloads and providing ongoing support for the success of my special education team.

As my commitment to building my capacity in special education grew, I also found myself encouraging and empowering the special education professionals to strengthen their voices as teacher leaders.

Through collaboration and empathy, we transformed challenges into opportunities. Teachers reported that they felt supported, balanced, and empowered and had a deep sense of belonging at our school. As the school years unfolded, I witnessed the impact of our collective efforts: inclusivity, utilization of resources, and celebrations of the success of all our staff and students.

—Christina Lucas-Sheffield, Principal, Arizona

 Takeaway Tool Kit

As we near the close of this chapter, I present three essential tools designed to streamline and enhance these processes. First, let me introduce you to the "Workload Analysis Tool" (figure 6.2, page 178). This tool aims to support you in gathering comprehensive input from teachers about their daily tasks and challenges. It includes a list of typical responsibilities, a daily task log, and sections for additional comments and suggestions, culminating in a summary and action plan. Be sure to add to it and adjust it however might be applicable for your context. By providing a clear picture of a teacher's workload, this tool aids in equitable task distribution and identifies areas where additional support is needed.

Workload Analysis Tool Template

To support you and your teams in gathering detailed input from special education teachers about their daily tasks and challenges, identify areas where additional support is needed and develop a more holistic understanding of their workload. This tool aims to ensure that tasks are distributed equitably and that teachers have the necessary resources and support to manage their responsibilities effectively.

Components:

Instructions for Use (adapt as needed)

1. Distribute the tool: Provide each special education teacher with a copy of the "Workload Analysis Tool."
2. Complete the sections: Instruct teachers to fill out the List of Typical Responsibilities, Daily Task Log, and Additional Comments and Suggestions sections over a specified period (for example, one week).
3. Collect and review: Collect the completed tools and review the information to identify common challenges and time-consuming tasks.
4. Develop an action plan: Use the Summary and Action Plan section to develop strategies for redistributing tasks, providing additional support, and addressing professional development needs.
5. Implement and monitor: Implement the action plan and regularly review progress to ensure the workload remains balanced and manageable.

List of Typical Responsibilities

Responsibility	Description	Time Spent (Hours/Week)	Additional Notes
IEP Documentation	Writing and updating Individualized Education Programs (IEPs) for students, including annual reviews and progress reports		
Instructional Planning	Developing lesson plans tailored to the unique needs of each student		
Behavioral Interventions	Creating and implementing Behavior Intervention Plans (BIPs), monitoring student behavior, and collecting data		
Direct Instruction	Providing instruction to students		
Co-Teaching	Collaborating with other teachers to deliver instruction in inclusive classroom settings using one of several co-teaching models		

Responsibility	Description	Time Spent (Hours/Week)	Additional Notes
Consultative Services	Consulting with general education teachers, parents, and other stakeholders to support student success		
Administrative Tasks	Completing paperwork, attending meetings, and other administrative duties		
Parent Communication	Regularly updating parents on student progress, involving them in the IEP process, and addressing concerns		
Professional Development	Participating in training sessions, workshops, and other professional development activities		
Case Management	Coordinating services for students, including scheduling meetings and ensuring compliance with legal and regulatory requirements		
Extracurricular Activities	Supervising or participating in extracurricular activities, such as after-school programs or clubs		

Daily Task Log

This tool can be amended as needed. Its intention is to help both you and your teachers track how time is spent in real time to effectively drive the workload optimization.

Date	Task	Description	Start Time	End Time	Total Time Spent	Comments
MM/DD/YY	IEP Documentation	Updated IEP for student A	8:00 a.m.	9:00 a.m.	1 hour	
MM/DD/YY	Instructional Planning	Developed lesson plan for the upcoming week	9:30 a.m.	11:00 a.m.	1.5 hours	
MM/DD/YY	Direct Instruction	Provided one-on-one reading intervention with student B	11:30 a.m.	12:00 p.m.	0.5 hours	
MM/DD/YY	Parent Communication	Called parents of student C to discuss progress	1:00 p.m.	1:30 p.m.	0.5 hours	
MM/DD/YY	Professional Development	Attended workshop on behavior management strategies	2:00 p.m.	4:00 p.m.	2 hours	

continued >

Figure 6.2: Workload analysis tool.

Additional Comments and Suggestions
- What challenges do you face in managing your workload?

- What tasks do you find most time-consuming?

- What support or resources would help you manage your workload more effectively?

- Do you have any other comments or suggestions?

Summary and Action Plan
- Top challenges identified:

- Most time-consuming tasks:

- Requested or necessary support or resources:

Action Plan
- Redistribution of tasks:

- Additional support staff required:

- Professional development needs:

- Changes to scheduling / time management:

Review and Follow-Up
- Next review date:

- Follow-up actions:

Visit **go.SolutionTree.com/specialneeds** for a free reproducible version of this figure.

The "Collaborative Success Plan (CSP) Template" (figure 6.3) offers a structured framework for setting and achieving professional growth goals. It emphasizes collaboration between administrators, teachers, and support staff, detailing specific actions, timelines, and resources required to meet these goals.

Teacher Information

Name: _____ Position: _____

Date: _____ School Leader: _____

Vision and Purpose
- **Vision statement:** Outline the overarching vision for the teacher's professional growth and success. You might co-create this with the teacher.
- **Purpose of the Collaborative Success Plan (CSP):** Explain the purpose of the CSP in fostering a collaborative and supportive environment.

Goals and Objectives

SMART Goal	Administrative Action	Teacher Action	Support Staff Action (if applicable)	Resources (if applicable)	Professional Learning Workshops (if applicable)	Timeline
Goal 1						
Goal 2						

Implementation Strategies
- Defined Roles and Responsibilities
  - Clearly identify and communicate the roles of everyone involved in the CSP.
  - Outline specific actions to be taken by the teacher, school leader, and other support personnel.
- Timely and Specific Feedback
  - Provide feedback immediately after experiencing relevant teaching practices.
  - Use things like classroom visits, email reviews, and conversations to deliver feedback.
- Visual and Verbal Feedback
  - Enhance feedback with visual aids like video clips from classroom visits, email exchanges, or checklists.
- Resource Identification and Timelines
  - Identify resources needed to support goals and set clear timelines for their provision.
  - Specify the support that will accompany these resources, such as training sessions or mentoring.

Progress Monitoring
- Review Meetings
  - Frequency—Schedule biweekly or monthly meetings.
  - Participants—Include all relevant personnel.
  - Agenda—Reflect on achievements, identify areas for improvement, and adjust strategies as needed.
- Data-Tracking Tools
  - Use digital platforms to monitor progress and visualize data with graphs and charts.
- Self-Reflection
  - Encourage teachers to engage in self-reflection with guiding questions.
- Documentation
  - Document all feedback and progress discussions in a transparent and accessible manner.
  - Include details on progress, feedback given, and agreed-on actions.

continued >

Figure 6.3: Collaborative Success Plan (CSP) template.

- Timely Adjustments
  - Make timely adjustments based on progress reviews.
  - Be flexible and willing to modify strategies as needed.

Recognition and Rewards

Achievements
- Goal 1: _____
- Goal 2: _____

Collective Commitment

Teacher
- Signature: _____ Date: _____

School Leader
- Signature: _____ Date: _____

Additional Support Personnel
- Signature: _____ Date: _____

*Visit **go.SolutionTree.com/special needs** for a free reproducible version of this figure.*

The "CSP Simple Progress Monitoring Tracker" (figure 6.4) is a straightforward tool for tracking the progress of set goals, documenting achievements, and determining next steps. These tools, adaptable to various school contexts, are designed to support school leaders in the continuous effort of teacher development, which crucially involves tracking data.

Goal	Date	Progress	Next Step	Date
Maintain progress monitoring tracker with up-to-date student data at least once each quarter.	September 30, 2024	No data entered to date. All data will be updated by next meeting. Shelly explained that she did not adequately prioritize this task and that the amount of data is overwhelming for her to be able to catch up. Support requested for data entry.	Leslie (paraprofessional) is assigned to support data entry.	October 15, 2024 (The Date columns repeat to correspond with the CSP meeting date.)

Figure 6.4: CSP simple progress monitoring tracker.

*Visit **go.SolutionTree.com/special needs** for a free reproducible version of this figure.*

 **Wrap-Up**

As we close the final chapter of this book, I cannot emphasize enough the importance of honoring the dedication and passion special education teachers bring to their roles each day. Your commitment to listening, supporting, and collaborating with your special education staff can transform their professional lives and enhance the educational experiences of their students. I have experienced this tale firsthand. This commitment should not be from just you alone; your entire leadership team (instructional coaches, department chairs, lead teachers, principals, coordinators, and so on) needs to embody these characteristics collectively.

By adopting these practices, you are showing your teachers that their well-being and professional growth matter. The insights and strategies I provided in this chapter are designed to support you in making informed decisions that enhance teacher satisfaction and effectiveness. Remember, the goal is to foster an environment where every special education teacher feels valued, supported, empowered, and equipped to provide the highest quality education for their students.

Epilogue

When I reflect on my journey into education, I see a path shaped by profound experiences and a calling to serve. As a teenager, my life was deeply impacted by witnessing my older brother's struggles—both in school and later in the criminal justice system. These moments led to my decision to study sociology and ignited a passion in me to create change, initially through criminal justice, but ultimately through education, where I realized I'd have the power to shape futures before challenges became insurmountable.

My transition into education was driven by the understanding that students thrive when they're surrounded by a network of support that includes caring, empowered, and effective educators. Educational leadership and special education have taught me that fostering success for students requires more than addressing their immediate needs—it demands a commitment to supporting the teachers who guide them daily. Teachers are not just facilitators of learning—they are builders of resilience, advocates of equity, and shapers of potential.

Through this book, my aim has been to emphasize a people-first approach to educational leadership. We cannot be so focused on student outcomes that we overlook or underestimate the importance of equipping teachers with the resources and support they need to succeed. When we care for our educators, we create the conditions for our students to flourish.

I leave you with this: The way forward is rooted in collaboration, thoughtful reflection, and an unwavering commitment to continuous improvement. Study the unique needs of your teachers and students, honor the expertise of your team, and remain open to learning alongside them. By fostering a culture of support and celebrating the contributions of every educator, we strengthen the foundation upon which student success is built.

Now that you've finished this book, I want to hear from you. I wrote this work in partnership with you—leaders, educators, and advocates—and in support of the students and teachers we serve. What topics would you like me to explore next? Perhaps there's a topic I discussed in this book you'd like to learn more about. Scan the QR code on this page to access a one-question survey where you can share your thoughts and suggestions. Your feedback will help shape my future projects so that together, we continue to advance the conversation and address the needs of our educational communities.

Thank you for your dedication to this vital work. You have the incredible opportunity to shape lives, transform systems, and build a future where all learners—students and teachers alike—can experience success.

References and Resources

Ansley, B. M., Houchins, D., & Varjas, K. (2019). Cultivating positive work contexts that promote teacher job satisfaction and retention in high-need schools. *Journal of Special Education Leadership*, *32*(1), 3–16.

Bain, C., Young, J., & Kuster, D. (2017). Finding the right fit: Three art teachers discover their mentorship style. *Art Education*, *70*(3), 29–33. https://doi.org/10.1080/00043125.2017.1286854

Baker, R., & Siemens, G. (2014). Educational data mining and learning analytics. In R. K. Sawyer (Ed.), *The Cambridge handbook of the learning sciences* (2nd ed., pp. 253–272). Cambridge University Press.

Bakken, J. P., & Obiakor, F. E. (Eds.). (2023). *Using technology to enhance special education: Vol. 37. Advances in special education.* Emerald. https://doi.org/10.1108/S0270-4013202337

Balta, N., Fukkink, R., & Amendum, S. J. (2023). The effect of job-embedded professional development on teacher and student outcomes: A multi-level meta-analysis. *International Educational Review*, *1*(1), 1–23. https://doi.org/10.58693/ier.111

Bandura, A. (1977). *Social learning theory*. Prentice Hall.

Berry, B., Darling-Hammond, L., & Mackay, A. (2021, October). *Teacher leadership for whole child education: A global perspective*. SC-TEACHER of the University of South Carolina. Accessed at https://sc-teacher.org/wp-content/uploads/2022/02/Teacher-Leadership-for-Whole-Child-Education-A-Global-Perspective_FINAL.pdf on February 3, 2025.

Billingsley, B., & Bettini, E. (2019). Special education teacher attrition and retention: A review of the literature. *Review of Educational Research*, *89*(5), 697–744. https://doi.org/10.3102/0034654319862495

Billingsley, B., Bettini, E., & Jones, N. D. (2019). Supporting special education teacher induction through high-leverage practices. *Remedial and Special Education*, *40*(6), 365–379.

Blad, E. (2024, May 13). Retention is the missing ingredient in special education staffing. *Education Week*. Accessed at www.edweek.org/leadership/retention-is-the-missing-ingredient-in-special-education-staffing/2024/05 on August 23, 2024.

Bronstein, L. R. (2002). Index of interdisciplinary collaboration. *Social Work Research*, *26*(2), 113–126. https://doi.org/10.1093/swr/26.2.113

Brunsting, N. C., Sreckovic, M. A., & Lane, K. L. (2014). Special education teacher burnout: A synthesis of research from 1979 to 2013. *Education and Treatment of Children*, *37*(4), 681–712.

Byrd, D. R., & Alexander, M. (2020). Investigating special education teachers' knowledge and skills: Preparing general teacher preparation for professional development. *Journal of Pedagogical Research*, *4*(2), 72–82. https://doi.org/10.33902/JPR.2020059790

CAST. (n.d.). *About the Guidelines 3.0 update*. Accessed at https://udlguidelines.cast.org/more/about-guidelines-3-0 on August 23, 2024.

Chanmugam, A., & Gerlach, B. (2013). A co-teaching model for developing future educators' teaching effectiveness. *International Journal of Teaching and Learning in Higher Education*, *25*(1), 110–117.

Cherner, T., & Smith, D. (2017). Reconceptualizing TPACK to meet the needs of twenty-first-century education. *The New Educator*, *13*(4), 329–349. https://doi.org/10.1080/1547688X.2015.1063744

Chitiyo, J., & Brinda, W. (2018). Teacher preparedness in the use of co-teaching in inclusive classrooms. *Support for Learning*, *33*(1), 38–51. https://doi.org/10.1111/1467-9604.12190

Clarke, D., & Hollingsworth, H. (2002). Elaborating a model of teacher professional growth. *Teaching and Teacher Education*, *18*(8), 947–967. https://doi.org/10.1016/s0742-051x(02)00053-7

Conzemius, A. E., & O'Neill, J. (2014). *The handbook for SMART school teams: Revitalizing best practices for collaboration* (2nd ed.). Solution Tree Press.

Cook, S. C., & McDuffie-Landrum, K. (2020). Integrating effective practices into co-teaching: Increasing outcomes for students with disabilities. *Intervention in School and Clinic*, *55*(4), 221–229. https://doi.org/10.1177/1053451219855739

Courduff, J., Szapkiw, A., & Wendt, J. L. (2016). Grounded in what works: Exemplary practice in special education teachers' technology integration. *Journal of Special Education Technology*, *31*(1), 26–38. https://doi.org/10.1177/0162643416633333

Covey, S. R. (2013). *The 7 habits of highly effective people: Powerful lessons in personal change* (25th anniversary ed.). Simon & Schuster.

Cox, E. (2015). Coaching and adult learning: Theory and practice. *New Directions for Adult and Continuing Education*, *2015*(148), 27–38.

Craig, M., & Kraemer, L. (2022). Technology as a classroom management asset. In J. Alcruz & M. Blair (Eds.), *Student-centered classrooms: Research-driven and inclusive strategies for classroom management* (pp. 153–172). Rowman & Littlefield.

Cranton, P., & Taylor, E. W. (2012). Transformative learning theory: Seeking a more unified theory. In E. W. Taylor & P. Cranton (Eds.), *The handbook of transformative learning: Theory, research, and practice* (pp. 3–20). Jossey-Bass.

Crawford, K., & Toledo, C. (2023). Help me before I quit! Reimagining new teacher mentoring programs. *The New Educator, 19*(3), 238–250. https://doi.org/10.1080/1547688X.2023.2223654

Criss, C. J., Konrad, M., Alber-Morgan, S. R., & Brock, M. E. (2024). A systematic review of goal setting and performance feedback to improve teacher practice. *Journal of Behavioral Education, 33*, 275–296. https://doi.org/10.1007/s10864-022-09494-1

Crouse, T., Rice, M., & Mellard, D. (2016, November). *"How did I survive?" Online teachers describe learning to teach students with disabilities.* Center on Online Learning and Students with Disabilities. Accessed at https://centerononlinelearning.ku.edu/wp-content/uploads/2017/04/HowDidISurvive-Nov2016.pdf on August 23, 2024.

Crouse, T., Rice, M., & Mellard, D. (2018). Learning to serve students with disabilities online: Teachers' perspectives. *Journal of Online Learning Research, 4*(2), 123–145.

Darling-Hammond, L. (2013). *Getting teacher evaluation right: What really matters for effectiveness and improvement.* Teachers College Press.

Darling-Hammond, L., Hyler, M. E., & Gardner, M. (2017, June). *Effective teacher professional development.* Learning Policy Institute. Accessed at https://learningpolicyinstitute.org/media/476/download?inline&file=Effective_Teacher_Professional_Development_REPORT.pdf on February 3, 2025.

Deschaine, M. (2018). *Supporting students with disabilities in K–12 online and blended learning.* Michigan Virtual University. Accessed at https://michiganvirtual.org/research/publications/supporting-students-with-disabilities-in-k-12-online-and-blended-learning on February 4, 2025.

Digital Learning Collaborative. (n.d.). *Proof Points Project.* Accessed at www.digitallearningcollab.com/proof-points-reports on February 3, 2025.

Digital Learning Collaborative. (2024). *Snapshot 2024: The post-pandemic digital learning landscape emerges.* Author.

Drago-Severson, E., & Pinto, K. C. (2006). School leadership for reducing teacher isolation: Drawing from the well of human resources. *International Journal of Leadership in Education, 9*(2), 129–155.

Eby, L. T., Allen, T. D., Evans, S. C., Ng, T., & DuBois, D. L. (2008). Does mentoring matter? A multidisciplinary meta-analysis comparing mentored and non-mentored individuals. *Journal of Vocational Behavior, 72*(2), 254–267.

Emery, D. W., & Vandenberg, B. (2010). Special education teacher burnout and ACT. *International Journal of Special Education, 25*(3), 119–131.

Every Student Succeeds Act, 20 U.S.C. § 6301 (2015).

Family Educational Rights and Privacy Act, 20 U.S.C. § 1232g (1974).

Felten, P., & Lambert, L. M. (2020). *Relationship-rich education: How human connections drive success in college*. Johns Hopkins University Press.

Frasier, A. S. (2022). What makes classroom observation feedback useful? The perceptions of secondary math and English teachers. *Voices of Reform: Educational Research to Inform and Reform, 5*(1), 40–58. https://doi.org/10.32623/5.00004

Fregni, J. (2023, June 16). *Mentorship helps educators find their path and purpose*. Accessed at www.teachforamerica.org/stories/power-of-mentorship on January 2, 2025.

Friend, M. (2008). Co-teaching: A simple solution that isn't simple after all. *Journal of Curriculum and Instruction, 2*(2), 9–19.

Friend, M. (2018). *Co-teach! Building and sustaining effective classroom partnerships in inclusive schools* (3rd ed.). Marilyn Friend.

Friend, M., & Barron, T. (2022). Collaborating with colleagues to increase student success. In J. McLeskey, L. Maheady, B. Billingsley, M. T. Brownell, & T. J. Lewis (Eds.), *High leverage practices for inclusive classrooms* (2nd ed., pp. 11–23). Routledge.

Friend, M., & Cook, L. (2007). *Interactions: Collaboration skills for school professionals* (5th ed.). Pearson.

Friend, M., & Cook, L. (2017). *Interactions: Collaboration skills for school professionals* (8th ed.). Pearson.

Friend, M., Cook, L., Hurley-Chamberlain, D., & Shamberger, C. (2010). Co-teaching: An illustration of the complexity of collaboration in special education. *Journal of Educational and Psychological Consultation, 20*(1), 9–27. https://doi.org/10.1080/10474410903535380

Fullan, M., & Edwards, M. (2022). *Spirit work and the science of collaboration*. Corwin Press.

Gately, S. E., & Gately, F. J. (2001). Understanding coteaching components. *TEACHING Exceptional Children, 33*(4), 40–47. https://doi.org/10.1177/004005990103300406

Gay, G. (2018). *Culturally responsive teaching: Theory, research, and practice* (3rd ed.). Teachers College Press.

Get News. (2023, December 20). Funding opportunity for iTrack software now accessible for all Michigan public and charter schools. *Observer News Enterprise*. Accessed at https://business.observernewsonline.com/observernewsonline/article/getnews-2023-12-20-funding-opportunity-for-itrack-software-now-accessible-for-all-michigan-public-and-charter-schools on February 5, 2025.

Goldman, S. R., Taylor, J., Carreon, A., & Smith, S. J. (2024). Using AI to support special education teacher workload. *Journal of Special Education Technology, 39*(3), 434–447.

Gonzalez, J. (2024). *The teacher's guide to tech 2024*. TPT. Accessed at www.teacherspayteachers.com/Product/The-Teachers-Guide-to-Tech-2024-10839098 on August 23, 2024.

Grimsby, R. (2020). "Anything is better than nothing!" Inservice teacher preparation for teaching students with disabilities. *Journal of Music Teacher Education, 29*(3), 77–90. https://doi.org/10.1177/1057083719893116

Hagaman, J. L., & Casey, K. J. (2018). Teacher attrition in special education: Perspectives from the field. *Teacher Education and Special Education, 41*(4), 277–291. https://doi.org/10.1177/0888406417725797

Hanover Research. (2018, December). *Best practices for teacher recruitment and retention.* Author. Accessed at www.schoolsalliance.com/wp-content/uploads/2019/01/Teacher-Recruitment-and-Retention-Best-Practices-1-3-2019-Southeast-Wisconsin-Schools-Alliance.pdf on February 4, 2025.

Hattie, J., & Timperley, H. (2007). The power of feedback. *Review of Educational Research, 77*(1), 81–112.

Henderson, S. L. (2014). *Factors that influence special education teacher retention* [Doctoral dissertation, Lindenwood University]. Digital Commons at Lindenwood University. https://digitalcommons.lindenwood.edu/dissertations/385

Hightower, A., Wiens, P., & Guzman, S. (2021). Formal mentorship and instructional practices: A Teaching and Learning International Survey (TALIS) study of US teachers. *International Journal of Mentoring and Coaching in Education, 10*(1), 118–132. https://doi.org/10.1108/ijmce-06-2020-0030

Holmes, W., Bialik, M., & Fadel, C. (2019). *Artificial intelligence in education: Promises and implications for teaching and learning.* Center for Curriculum Redesign.

Huberman, M., Navo, M., & Parrish, T. (2012). Effective practices in high performing districts serving students in special education. *Journal of Special Education Leadership, 25*(2), 59–71.

Individuals with Disabilities Education Act, 20 U.S.C. § 1400 (2004).

Individuals with Disabilities Education Act, 34 CFR § 300.101 (2004). Accessed at https://sites.ed.gov/idea/regs/b/b/300.101 on February 4, 2025.

Individuals with Disabilities Education Act, 34 CFR § 300.39 (2004). Accessed at https://sites.ed.gov/idea/regs/b/a/300.39 on February 4, 2025.

Individuals with Disabilities Education Act, 34 CFR § 300.8 (2004). Accessed at https://sites.ed.gov/idea/regs/b/a/300.8 on February 4, 2025.

International Society for Technology in Education. (2023). *ISTE Standards.* Accessed at https://iste.org/standards on February 4, 2025.

Irwin, V., Wang, K., Jung, J., Kessler, E., Tezil, T., Alhassani, S., et al. (2024). *Report on the condition of education 2024* (NCES 2024-144). U.S. Department of Education. Accessed at https://nces.ed.gov/pubs2024/2024144.pdf on February 4, 2025.

Juniper Education. (2023, October 16). *10 ways to reduce teacher workload in schools* [Blog post]. Accessed at https://junipereducation.org/blog/10-ways-to-reduce-teacher-workload-in-schools on August 23, 2024.

Kennedy, M. M. (2016). How does professional development improve teaching? *Review of Educational Research, 86*(4), 945–980.

King-Sears, M. E., Jenkins, M. C., & Brawand, A. (2020). Co-teaching perspectives from middle school algebra co-teachers and their students with and without disabilities. *International Journal of Inclusive Education, 24*(4), 427–442. https://doi.org/10.1080/13603116.2018.1465134

Kobischen, E. E. (2020). *Collaboration and the intent to stay: A quantitative correlational study of special education teachers in Maine* [Doctoral dissertation, Grand Canyon University]. ProQuest Dissertations & Theses. www.proquest.com/dissertations-theses/collaboration-intent-stay-quantitative/docview/2331812915/se-2

Konrad, M., Keesey, S., Ressa, V. A., Alexeeff, M., Chan, P. E., & Peters, M. T. (2014). Setting clear learning targets to guide instruction for all students. *Intervention in School and Clinic, 50*(2), 76–85.

Kumar, V. (2020). Data-driven decision making in education: Using data to improve teaching and learning. In P. D. Moskal, C. D. Dziuban, & A. G. Picciano (Eds.), *Data analytics and adaptive learning: Research perspectives* (pp. 1–19). Routledge.

Levin, J., Berg-Jacobson, A., Atchison, D., Lee, K., & Vontsolos, E. (2015, December). *Massachusetts study of teacher supply and demand: Trends and projections.* American Institutes for Research. Accessed at www.air.org/sites/default/files/2021-06/Massachusetts-Study-of-Teacher-Supply-and-Demand-December-2015_rev.pdf on February 4, 2025.

Lewis, C. (2015). What is improvement science? Do we need it in education? *Educational Researcher, 44*(1), 54–61. https://doi.org/10.3102/0013189X15570388

Mathew, P., Mathew, P., & Peechattu, J. (2017). Reflective practices: A means to teacher development. *Asia Pacific Journal of Contemporary Education and Communication Technology, 3*(1), 126–131.

Muhammad, A. (2009). *Transforming school culture: How to overcome staff division.* Solution Tree Press.

Muhammad, A. (2018). *Transforming school culture: How to overcome staff division* (2nd ed.). Solution Tree Press.

Muhammad, A. (2024). *The way forward: PLC at Work and the bright future of education.* Solution Tree Press.

Murawski, W. W. (2010). *Collaborative teaching in elementary schools: Making the co-teaching marriage work!* Corwin Press.

Murawski, W. W., & Lee Swanson, H. (2001). A meta-analysis of co-teaching research: Where are the data? *Remedial and Special Education, 22*(5), 258–267.

National Association of Secondary School Principals. (2021, July). *Supporting principals as leaders of special education.* Author. Accessed at www.nassp.org/resource/supporting-principals-as-leaders-of-special-education on August 23, 2024.

National Center for Education Statistics. (2020). *Teacher induction and mentoring: Findings from the National Teacher and Principal Survey.* U.S. Department of Education. Accessed at https://nces.ed.gov/surveys/ntps/ on January 10, 2025.

National Center for Education Statistics. (2024). *Students with disabilities.* Accessed at https://nces.ed.gov/programs/coe/indicator/cgg/students-with-disabilities on February 4, 2025.

National Institute for Excellence in Teaching. (2012, March). *Beyond "job-embedded": Ensuring that good professional development gets results.* Author. Accessed at www.niet.org/assets/ResearchAndPolicyResources/688a72b19e/beyond_job_embedded_professional_development.pdf on February 4, 2025.

Nelson, L. L. (2019). *Design and deliver: Planning and teaching using Universal Design for Learning* (2nd ed.). Brookes.

Network for Educator Effectiveness. (n.d.). *Writing and implementing effective Performance Improvement Plans (PIPs).* Accessed at https://neeadvantage.com/pip on August 23, 2024.

Network for Educator Effectiveness. (2022). *Guide to effective teacher performance improvement plans.* Author. Accessed at https://neeadvantage.com/wp-content/uploads/2022/09/NEE-Guide-to-Effective-Teacher-Performance-Improvement-Plans-PIP.pdf on February 4, 2025.

Nichols, H. (2024, November 1). *How to support teachers' emotional health.* Accessed at www.edutopia.org/article/supporting-teachers-emotional-health on February 3, 2025.

No Child Left Behind Act of 2001, Pub. L. No. 107-110, § 115 Stat. 1425 (2002).

Olechowska, A. (2020). The student through Bronfenbrenner's "glasses"—Teachers' knowledge of students with special educational needs from a micro- and mesosystemic perspective. *Pedagogical Contexts, 2*(15), 241–259. https://doi.org/10.19265/kp.2020.2.15.280

Ortan, F., Simut, C., & Simut, R. (2021). Self-efficacy, job satisfaction and teacher well-being in the K–12 educational system. *International Journal of Environmental Research and Public Health, 18*(23), Article 12763. https://doi.org/10.3390/ijerph182312763

Park, E.-Y., & Shin, M. (2020). A meta-analysis of special education teachers' burnout. *SAGE Open, 10*(2).

Passow, A. (2019, January 3). How K–12 schools have adopted artificial intelligence. *EdTech: Focus on K–12.* Accessed at https://edtechmagazine.com/k12/article/2019/01/how-k-12-schools-have-adopted-artificial-intelligence on February 4, 2025.

Prizeman, R. (2021). Perspectives on the co-teaching experience: Examining the views of teaching staff and students. *REACH: Journal of Inclusive Education in Ireland, 29*(1), 43–53.

Radu, I. (2014). Augmented reality in education: A meta-review and cross-media analysis. *Personal and Ubiquitous Computing, 18,* 1533–1543.

Rice, M. F., & Dykeman, B. (2014). The emerging research base on online learning and students with disabilities. In K. Kennedy & R. E. Ferdig (Eds.), *Handbook of research on K–12 online and blended learning* (2nd ed., pp. 189-206). ETC Press.

Robinson, O., Bridges, S., & Rollins, L. (2017, April 19–22). *Preventing the teacher failure cycle* [Conference presentation]. Council for Exceptional Children 2017 Convention & Expo, Boston, MA, United States.

Robinson, O., Bridges, S., Rollins, L., & Schumacker, R. E. (2019). A study of the relation between special education burnout and job satisfaction. *Journal of Research in Special Educational Needs, 19*(4), 295–303.

Rodman, A. (2019). *Personalized professional learning: A job-embedded pathway for elevating teacher voice.* ASCD.

Scott, L. A., Taylor, J. P., Bruno, L., Padhye, I., Brendli, K., Wallace, W., et al. (2022). Why do they stay? Factors associated with special education teachers' persistence. *Remedial and Special Education, 43*(2), 75–86. https://doi.org/10.1177/07419325211014965

Seppala, E. (2014, May 8). *Connectedness & health: The science of social connection.* Accessed at https://ccare.stanford.edu/uncategorized/connectedness-health-the-science-of-social-connection on August 24, 2024.

Shen, B., McCaughtry, N., Martin, J., Garn, A., Kulik, N., & Fahlman, M. (2015). The relationship between teacher burnout and student motivation. *British Journal of Educational Psychology, 85*(4), 519–532.

Sheninger, E. (2019). *Digital leadership: Changing paradigms for changing times* (2nd ed.). Corwin Press.

Sheppard, M. E., & Wieman, R. (2020). What do teachers need? Math and special education teacher educators' perceptions of essential teacher knowledge and experience. *The Journal of Mathematical Behavior, 59,* Article 100798. https://doi.org/10.1016/j.jmathb.2020.100798

Siyam, N. (2019). Factors impacting special education teachers' acceptance and actual use of technology. *Education and Information Technologies, 24*(3), 2035–2057. https://doi.org/10.1007/s10639-018-09859-y

Slagg, A. (2024, August 19). How generative AI improves parent engagement in K–12 schools. *EdTech: Focus on K–12.* Accessed at https://edtechmagazine.com/k12/article/2024/08/how-generative-ai-improves-parent-engagement-k-12-schools-perfcon on February 4, 2025.

Smith, D. (2021). The role of AI in special education. *Journal of Special Education Technology, 36*(1), 5–10.

Smith, T. M., & Ingersoll, R. M. (2004). What are the effects of induction and mentoring on beginning teacher turnover? *American Educational Research Journal, 41*(3), 681–714.

State Support Network. (2018). Needs assessment guidebook. Accessed at www.ed.gov/sites/ed/files/2020/10/needsassessmentguidebook-508_003.pdf on March 25, 2025.

Stewart-Banks, B., Kuofie, M., Hakim, A., & Branch, R. (2015). Education leadership styles impact on work performance and morale of staff. *Journal of Marketing and Management, 6*(2), 87–105.

Strogilos, V., & King-Sears, M. E. (2019). Co-teaching is extra help and fun: Perspectives on co-teaching from middle school students and co-teachers. *Journal of Research in Special Educational Needs, 19*(2), 92–102. https://doi.org/10.1111/1471-3802.12427

Stufflebeam, D. L., McCormick, C. H., Brinkerhoff, R. O., & Nelson, C. O. (1985). *Conducting educational needs assessments*. Kluwer-Nijhoff.

Sweigart, C. A., & Landrum, T. J. (2015). The impact of number of adults on instruction: Implications for co-teaching. *Preventing School Failure: Alternative Education for Children and Youth*, *59*(1), 22–29.

Tahir, K., Doelger, B., & Hynes, M. (2019). A case study on the ecology of inclusive education in the United States. *Journal for Leadership and Instruction*, *18*(1), 17–24.

Taylor, E. S., & Tyler, J. H. (n.d.). *The effect of evaluation on teacher performance*. Accessed at https://scholar.harvard.edu/files/evaluation-performance-tt.pdf on August 23, 2024.

Theobald, R. J., Goldhaber, D. D., Naito, N., & Stein, M. L. (2021). The special education teacher pipeline: Teacher preparation, workforce entry, and retention. *Exceptional Children*, *88*(1), 65–80.

Tracy-Bronson, C. P. (2020). District-level inclusive special education leaders demonstrate social justice strategies. *Journal of Special Education Leadership*, *33*(2), 59–77.

Trembley, P. (2013). Collaborative teaching in inclusive classrooms: Making the co-teaching marriage work! *International Journal of Special Education*, *28*(3), 1–12.

U.S. Department of Education. (n.d.). *About IDEA*. Accessed at https://sites.ed.gov/idea/about-idea/#IDEA-History on August 23, 2024.

Wall, B. C. (2023). *Achievement of online school students with specific learning disabilities: A focus on knowledge, pedagogy, and preparation of online general and special education teachers* [Unpublished doctoral dissertation]. Johns Hopkins University.

Wall, B. C. (2024). Preparedness of online general and special educators to teach diverse learners: A study of online middle school teachers' perceptions. *Journal of Online Learning Research*, *10*(1), 113–148.

Weerts, M. (2020). *Co-teaching: Benefits and challenges of co-teaching in middle school* [Doctoral dissertation, St. Cloud State University]. The Repository at St. Cloud State. https://repository.stcloudstate.edu/edad_etds/72

Wexler, J., Kearns, D. M., Lemons, C. J., Mitchell, M., Clancy, E., Davidson, K. A., et al. (2018). Reading comprehension and co-teaching practices in middle school English language arts classrooms. *Exceptional Children*, *84*(4), 384–402. https://doi.org/10.1177/0014402918771543

White, M. (2024, January 8). Transitioning to a workload approach in K–12 special education. *eSchool News*. Accessed at www.eschoolnews.com/innovative-teaching/2024/01/08/workload-approach-k-12-special-education on February 5, 2025.

Wickramaratne, P. J., Yangchen, T., Lepow, L., Patra, B. G., Glicksburg, B., Talati, A., et al. (2022). Social connectedness as a determinant of mental health: A scoping review. *PLOS One*, *17*(10), Article e0275004. https://doi.org/10.1371/journal.pone.0275004

Wilkins, E. L. (2022). *A program evaluation of the Marilyn Friend co-teaching models* [Doctoral dissertation, Gardner-Webb University]. Digital Commons at Gardner-Webb University. https://digitalcommons.gardner-webb.edu/education-dissertations/106

Will, M. (2017, June 22). Mentors for new teachers found to boost student achievement—by a lot. *Education Week*. Accessed at www.edweek.org/leadership/mentors-for-new-teachers-found-to-boost-student-achievement-by-a-lot/2017/06 on February 4, 2025.

Willis, C. B., Bruno, L. P., Scott, L. A., & Bateman, D. F. (2022). Identifying the least restrictive environment. In J. A. Rodriguez & W. W. Murawski (Eds.), *Special education law and policy: From foundation to application* (pp. 327–360). Plural.

Wilson, G. L. (2016). *Co-planning for co-teaching: Time-saving routines that work in inclusive classrooms*. ASCD.

Zagona, A. L., Kurth, J. A., & MacFarland, S. Z. C. (2017). Teachers' views of their preparation for inclusive education and collaboration. *Teacher Education and Special Education, 40*(3), 163–178. https://doi.org/10.1177/0888406417692969

Zeidner, M., Matthews, G., & Roberts, R. D. (2009). *What we know about emotional intelligence: How it affects learning, work, relationships, and our mental health*. MIT Press.

Zimmer, W. K., & Matthews, S. D. (2022). A virtual coaching model of professional development to increase teachers' digital learning competencies. *Teaching and Teacher Education, 109*, Article 103544. https://doi.org/10.1016/j.tate.2021.103544

Index

A

academic performance data, 97. *See also* data
accessibility and co-planning, 78
accommodations, 103–104
adaptability, 113
administrative work, 159
adult learning strategies, 19
AI in special education. *See also* leveraging digital tools, assistive technology, and AI
    about, 136–137
    adjustments in teaching strategies and, 140
    administrative efficiency and teacher support and, 138–139
    data-driven decision making and, 139–140
    ethical considerations and benefits of, 140–141
    personalized learning and IEPs, 137–138
    student engagement and collaboration and, 139
alternative communication, 113. *See also* communication
alternative teaching models, 73–74. *See also* co-teaching
assessments
    assessment checklists, 61–62
    assessment cycles, 52. *See also* continuous evaluation
    assessment schedules, 61
asynchronous training tools, 55–56
asynchronous videos, 127–129

B

Bass, R., 7
behavior
    behavioral data, 97
    behavioral development, 112–113
    behavioral interventions, 157
    behavior tracking, 126, 150
brainstorming sessions, 77, 99–100. *See also* co-planning
budget allocation, 69, 141

C

celebrations
    celebrating successes, 29
    collaborative success plans and, 175
    co-teaching models and, 70
    optimizing workload management and performance improvement and, 176
    pre-IEP meeting steps and, 99
check-ins and IEP meetings, 102

coaching
- about, 46–47
- active coaching and support guide, 47–48
- co-teaching models and, 69
- ongoing professional learning framework and, 39
- virtual coaching, 56

collaboration
- collaborative planning guide, 149–150
- collective pedagogy and, 63–65
- co-teaching models and, 69
- enhanced virtual communication and, 135–136
- fostering a culture of, 176
- interactive workshops and, 43
- post-IEP meeting steps, 104
- technology and strategies for optimizing workloads, 166

collaborative success plans (CSPs)
- about, 171
- CSP simple progress monitoring tracker, 182
- template for, 181–182
- transforming performance improvement into success plans, 171–175

collective pedagogy, 63–65

communication
- AI-powered communication tools, 139
- alternative communication, 113
- asynchronous videos and, 127–129
- coaching and support and, 46
- communication development, 113
- continuous evaluation and, 52
- co-teaching and co-planning and, 80
- co-teaching models and, 68
- digital class ecosystems and, 129–131
- enhanced virtual communication and collaboration, 135–136
- IEPs and, 104, 105
- instant notifications, 126–127
- mentor training and, 18
- prioritizing transparent communication, 28–29
- technologies for, 124–131

community and belonging, 14

compensation, 3

compliance, 112

connections
- cultivating a culture of, 28
- human connections, 7
- impact of, 7–8
- understanding the power of, 27

continuous evaluation, 39, 52–54. *See also* ongoing professional learning framework

co-planning
- about, 75–76
- collaborative planning guide, 149–150
- co-teaching planning tool, 90
- fostering effective co-planning, 77–79
- importance of, 76–77
- job-embedded training and, 54–55
- mentorship and, 12
- promoting collaborative planning, 161–162
- quick guide for collaborative planning sessions, 163–164
- reflection questions for equitable co-planning, 85

co-teaching
- about, 65–67
- attributes of an effective co-teaching model, 67–71
- co-teaching action checklist, 88–89
- co-teaching models, 71–75
- co-teaching planning tool, 90
- high-leverage practices and, 12
- job-embedded training and, 54–55
- reflection questions for co-teaching implementation, 86
- reflection questions when considering co-teaching for the first time, 84
- roles and responsibilities of, 78–79, 80
- voices from the field, 81–83

co-teaching and co-planning

about, 63–65
co-planning, 75–79
co-teaching, 65–75
takeaway tool kit, 83–90
tips from the top, 80–81
voices from the field, 81–83
wrap-up, 91
creative expression stations, 73. *See also* station teaching models
cultural competence and mentor training, 19
culture of continuous learning, 14

D

data
academic performance data, 97
behavioral data, 97
data privacy concerns, 142
data-driven decision making, 139–140
needs assessments and, 40, 41
optimizing workload management and performance improvement, 175
pre-IEP meeting steps and, 97–98, 100–101
specialized data, 97
documentation
collaborative success plans and, 174
IEPs and, 95, 105, 159
technologies to support, 132–133

E

emotional intelligence, 19, 29
emotional regulation, 112
emotional support, 10, 11, 176
empathy, 28, 112
evaluation and co-teaching, 70. *See also* continuous evaluation; co-teaching
expressive language, 113. *See also* communication

F

families
communication and, 125, 136
digital class ecosystems and, 130–131
family input forms, 99, 117–118
IEPs and, 95–96
instant notifications and, 126–127
feedback
collaborative success plans and, 173
communication and, 28
co-planning and, 79
digital class ecosystem, 131
feedback integration meetings, 52
IEP meeting steps and, 98, 100, 104
IEP reviews and, 105
instant notifications and, 127
mentorship and, 10, 18
optimizing workloads and, 163–164, 166
fine motor skills, 113

G

general education teachers. *See also* co-teaching and co-planning; special education teachers
collective pedagogy and, 64–65
legislation and accountability and, 65
teacher efficacy and job satisfaction, 14–15
goals
collaborative success plans and, 172
co-planning and, 77–78
IEP goal progress monitoring form, 119
needs assessments and, 41
SMART goals, 41, 78
gross motor skills, 113

H

health considerations, 113
high-leverage practices (HLPs), 10, 11–12
human connections, 7. *See also* connections

I

IEPs (individualized education plans). *See also* preparing and implementing collaborative IEPs
about, 93–94
and AI in special education, 137–138
elements of, 94–96

family input forms, 117–118
and general education classes, 1
IEP goal progress monitoring form, 119
IEP reviews, 105–106
meeting process for, 96
meetings, scenarios for, 106–109
post-IEP meeting steps, 96, 102–106
pre-IEP group feedback form, 114–115
pre-IEP meeting steps, 96, 97–101
technology to support, 133
workload management and, 157–159
implementation
   coaching and support and, 46
   collaborative success plans and, 172–173
   digital class ecosystems and, 130
individualized instruction, 157
information sharing, 28
in-person learning, 74, 75
instant notifications, 126–127
interactive workshops. *See also* ongoing professional learning framework
   about, 42–44, 46
   interactive workshop planning guide, 44–45
   ongoing professional learning framework and, 39
introduction
   special education, perception and workload of, 1–2
   what's in this book, 4–6
   why I wrote this book, 2–3
investing in professional learning. *See also* professional development
   about, 37–38
   assessment checklists, 61–62
   assessment schedules, 61
   job-embedded training and, 54–57
   ongoing professional learning framework, 38–54
   takeaway tool kit, 60
   tips from the top, 57–59
   voices from the field, 59–60
   wrap-up, 60–62
isolation, xii–xiv

J
job-embedded training, 54–57. *See also* professional development
journaling, 49

L
leadership
   co-planning and, 76–77
   co-teaching models and, 68, 69
   technology integration guide for school leaders, 147–148
   workload management and, 167–168
learning stations, 72–73. *See also* station teaching models
legislation and legalities, 95, 158
leveraging digital tools, assistive technology, and AI
   about, 123–124
   AI in special education, 136–141
   collaborative planning guide, 149–150
   empowering progress through reflection, 145–147
   introductory resource list, 151–153
   takeaway tool kit, 144–153
   technologies for effective communication, 124–131
   technologies to support documentation storage and project management, 132–136
   technology integration guide for school leaders, 147–148
   technology integration in special education, 131–132
   tips from the top, 141–142
   voices from the field, 142–143
   wrap-up, 154

M
meetings
   feedback integration meetings, 52

high-leverage practices and, 12
meeting process for IEPs, 96
post-IEP meeting steps, 96, 102–106
pre-IEP meeting steps, 96, 97–101
reflective practice and, 49
scenarios for IEP meetings, 106–109
virtual meetings, 135
mentorship
assignment of, 9
example anonymous mentorship program feedback survey, 20–21
example mentor-mentee pairing questionnaire, 17–18
example mentorship program design worksheet, 24–26
feedback mechanisms and, 19
implications for special education, 10–15
importance of, 9
improving relationships and culture through, 9–26
mentor and mentee matching, 15–18
mentor approach, 13
mentor training, 18–19
program design and, 23
programs, structure of mentorship programs, 9–10
recognition and incentives for participation, 22
sustainability planning, 22
technology and, 21
tips from the top, 29
voices from the field, 30–31

N

needs assessments
about, 40–42
needs assessment starter reflection guide, 42
ongoing professional learning framework and, 39
optimizing workloads and, 166
professional development and, 58
workshops and, 43

O

observation and feedback, 10, 49, 55. *See also* feedback
one teach, one assist model, 71–72. *See also* co-teaching
one teach, one observe model, 75. *See also* co-teaching
ongoing professional learning framework. *See also* investing in professional learning
about, 38–40
coaching and support and, 46–48
continuous evaluation and, 52–54
interactive workshops and, 42–46
needs assessments and, 40–42
reflective practice and, 49–51
online learning, 74, 75
open dialogue, 27. *See also* communication
optimizing workload management and performance improvement. *See also* project management
about, 155–156
collaborative success plan template, 181–182
CSP simple progress monitoring tracker, 182
performance improvement and collaborative success plans, 169–175
strategies for optimizing workloads, 159–168
takeaway tool kit, 177–182
tips from the top, 175–176
voices from the field, 176–177
workload analysis tool, 178–180
workload management, 156–159
wrap-up, 183

P

peer collaboration stations, 73. *See also* station teaching models
peer sharing circles, 49
performance improvement plans (PIPs)

about, 169–170
cultivating a leadership mindset, 170–171
transforming performance improvement into success plans, 171–175
physical development, 113
Plan-Do-Study-Act cycle, 67
planning time, 70. *See also* co-planning
post-IEP meeting steps. *See also* IEPs (individualized education plans)
scenario for in-person meetings, 108
scenario for virtual meetings, 108–109
steps for, 102–106
pre-IEP meeting steps. *See also* IEPs (individualized education plans)
pre-IEP group feedback form, 114–115
scenario for in-person meetings, 106–107
scenario for virtual meetings, 107–108
steps for, 97–101
preparing and implementing collaborative IEPs. *See also* IEPs (individualized education plans)
about, 93–94
navigating the complexities of IEPs, 94–109
takeaway tool kit, 111–120
tips from the top, 109–110
voices from the field, 110–111
wrap-up, 121
professional development. *See also* investing in professional learning; ongoing professional learning framework
administrative efficiency and teacher support and, 138–139
co-teaching and co-planning and, 80–81
co-teaching models and, 69
digital class ecosystems and, 130
IEP meetings and, 100
impact on special education teachers, 37–38
job-embedded training and, 54–57
leveraging digital tools, assistive technology, and AI, 142
mentorship programs and, 9–10

tips from the top, 29
workload management and, 166, 167, 175
progress monitoring
AI and, 139
collaborative success plans and, 173–174
CSP simple progress monitoring tracker, 182
digital class ecosystems and, 131
IEP goal progress monitoring form, 119
IEPs and, 95, 104
project management. *See also* optimizing workload management and performance improvement
insights for, 134–135
technologies to support, 132–136

R

real-time communication. *See* communication
receptive language, 113. *See also* communication
recognition and rewards, 175
reflection and reflective practice. *See also* ongoing professional learning framework
about, 49
empowering progress through reflection, 145–147
high-leverage practices and, 12
ongoing professional learning framework and, 39, 49–51
post-IEP meeting steps and, 104
reflection and post-learning action guide, 50–51
relationship management, 158. *See also* connections
resources
co-teaching and co-planning and, 81
co-teaching models and, 68–69
introductory resource list, 150–153
pre-IEP meeting steps and, 99
retaining special educators through systems of support
about, 7–9
actionable insights worksheet for leadership

success, 32–34
communication, building bridges through, 27–28
connections, understanding the power of, 27
mentorship, improving relationships and culture with, 9–26
takeaway tool kit, 31
tips from the top, 28–29
voices from the field, 29–31
wrap-up, 35

S

self-concept, 112
self-control, 112
self-efficacy, teacher efficacy and job satisfaction, 14–15
self-observation, 49
self-reflection, 174, 176
small-group instruction, 71, 73
SMART goals, 41, 78. *See also* goals
social communication, 113. *See also* communication
social skills, 112
social-emotional data, 97
social-emotional development, 112
special education teachers. *See also* co-teaching and co-planning; retaining special educators through systems of support
    collective pedagogy and, 63–65
    teacher efficacy and job satisfaction, 14–15
    job satisfaction and, 1–2, 3
specialized data, 97. *See also* data
specially designed instruction, definition of, 12–13
stakeholder engagement and pre-IEP meeting steps, 98–99
station teaching models, 72–73. *See also* co-teaching
structured observations, 55
students
    AI and student engagement and collaboration, 139
    identifying and addressing student needs in co-planning, 78
    IEPs and student profiles, 94–95
    privacy and, 125, 142

T

targeted support, 13–14
teachers
    co-teachers. *See* co-teaching and co-planning
    general education teachers. *See* general education teachers
    special education teachers. *See* special education teachers
    teacher efficacy and job satisfaction, 14–15
team teaching models, 74. *See also* co-teaching
technology. *See also* leveraging digital tools, assistive technology, and AI
    IEPs and, 110
    introductory resource list, 150–153
    post-IEP meeting steps and, 102
    pre-IEP group feedback forms and, 115–116
    pre-IEP meeting steps and, 101
    resistance to change and, 141–142
    strategies for optimizing workloads, 165–167
    technology integration guide for school leaders, 147–148
    technology integration stations, 73
time
    planning time, 70. *See also* co-planning
    training in time management, 164–165

U

Universal Design for Learning (UDL), 69

V

videos, asynchronous video, 127–129
virtual coaching, 56
virtual meetings, 135

W

workload analysis tool, 178–180

workload management
- about, 156–159
- caseload approaches, transitioning from to workload approaches to, 160–161
- collaborative planning and, 161–164
- feedback and support and, 163–164
- insights for, 134–135
- leadership support and, 167–168
- ongoing professional learning and, 167
- technology and software, leveraging, 165–167
- time management, training in, 164–165

workshops. *See also* interactive workshops
- reflective practice and, 49
- voices from the field, 59–60

Co-Teaching Evolved
Matthew Rhoads and Belinda Dunnick Karge

The authors offer a revived approach to co-teaching that accounts for pressing topics in today's classroom. PreK–12 teachers will learn to create collaborative co-teaching partnerships and navigate key co-teaching components—such as lesson design, conflict resolution, and communication with stakeholders—with research-backed tools and strategies.

BKG202

Watch, Listen, Ask, Learn
Belinda Dunnick Karge

Written for current and aspiring administrators and teacher leaders, this book offers action items, case studies, and reproducible tools to help you stay in front of special education law, know and support your learning services team, and ensure students with disabilities receive equitable, inclusive education.

BKG080

The Collaborative IEP
Kristen M. Bordonaro and Megan Clarke

In this guide, discover the essential steps and vital understandings for team members to create student-centered IEPs. This book simplifies the IEP writing process and provides practical strategies and structures that can help all educators create compliant and effective IEPs for students.

BKG122

The ADMIRE Framework for Inclusion
Toby J. Karten

Create successful inclusion classrooms with a framework that strengthens self-efficacy and equips teachers to be their best in accommodating students with diverse abilities and cultivating supportive relationships among teachers, students, and their families. This book shares evidence-based practices and strategies field-tested by inclusion professionals.

BKG174

Solution Tree | Press

a division of Solution Tree

Visit SolutionTree.com or call 800.733.6786 to order.

We don't just help schools make a change, we help them *be* the change

REAL IMPACT. RELEVANT SOLUTIONS. RESULTS-DRIVEN APPROACH.

From funding to faculty retention, the evolving demands schools face can be overwhelming. That's where we come in. With professional development rooted in decades of research and delivered by many of the educators who literally wrote the book on it, we empower schools to achieve meaningful change with real, sustainable results.

The change starts here. We can make it happen together.

See how we can get real results for your school or district.

Scan the code or visit:
SolutionTree.com/Results-Driven

 Solution Tree   LET'S SEE WHAT **WE CAN** DO TOGETHER